T0308790

ÁGUILA

ÁGUILA

The Vision, Life, Death & Rebirth of a Two-Spirit Shaman in the Ozark Mountains

María Cristina Moroles
Lauri Umansky

The University of Arkansas Press
Fayetteville
2024

The names and other identifying characteristics of some people have been changed to protect their privacy.

978-1-68226-243-6 (cloth)
978-1-61075-807-9 (electronic)

28 27 26 25 24   5 4 3 2 1

Manufactured in the United States of America

Designed by Daniel Bertalotto

♾ The paper used in this publication meets the minimum requirements of the American National Standard for Permanence of Paper for Printed Library Materials Z39.48–1984.

Frontispiece: *The Call*, color-pencil drawing by Liliana Wilson, 2020. Image courtesy of the artist.

Cataloging-in-Publication Data on file at the Library of Congress.

To our unconditionally loving Tierra Madre Tonantzin / Mother Earth.

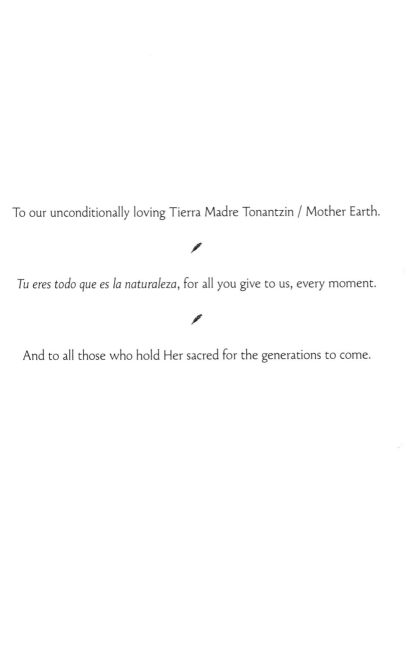

Tu eres todo que es la naturaleza, for all you give to us, every moment.

And to all those who hold Her sacred for the generations to come.

Contents

Acknowledgments
ix

🪶

Prayer for Águila
3

1 Awakening
5

2 Madre
9

3 Dallas: House
13

4 Dallas: Street
27

5 Dallas: Vision
37

6 O Arkansas!
49

7 SunHawk
59

8 This Land Is Our Land
67

9 Drama in These Hills
71

10 Growing *La Familia*
77

11 Love and Loss
91

12 Tonantzin, Mother Earth
99

13 New Life
107

14 Back to the Land
119

15 Heartbreak and Healing
125

16 Águila
133

17 To the Womb of Our Mother
139

18 Home
153

Afterword
157

Selected Bibliography
169

Acknowledgments

To my first teachers—my parents, María Bautista Moroles and José Elizondo Moroles—for all their love and support and their wisdom in teaching me survival skills that helped me navigate the changing currents this River of Life brings.

Special gratitude to my dear children, Jennifer Jo Moroles and Mario Solano DeColores, for your love and your generosity in sharing your lives with me and the hundreds of people who have come to this land and into our lives seeking healing and sanctuary. Thank you for teaching me with your beauty, patience, innocence, compassion, and courage. You too have been my teachers. You are my heart and our future.

Gratitude to Águila/Eagle medicine, which helps me see from high above to live from my highest self; to all the four-legged animals that teach me to walk gently upon my Mother; and to the finned ones that teach me to be One with the flow of Life.

Tlatzokamati to Cynthia Pérez, *por la cabrona que eres*, for without your continual nagging to write this book, it might never have seen the light of day; and to my big sister of the heart, Juanita Arriega Frost. Gracias to you both for your availability as *hermanas*, *amigas*, and *consejeras*; in spite of your personal, spiritual, and community-service obligations, and your political lives, you always made time for me, especially in moments of need. Gracias for caring for me with your limitless generosity, for driving me around the city, for helping me navigate airport comings and goings, for scheduling massages and acupuncture to help keep me going, for hosting me in your homes at a moment's notice, and for unconditionally, lovingly supporting me. You were both harbors and anchors for me as I took to the road in my beat-up vehicles with little or no money for my visits from the land, south to Texas to spend time with *mi familia* or to go on another spiritual journey. *Tlatzokamati, hermanas, las amo y las respeto hasta siempre.*

Tlatzokamati a los espíritus y los antepasados de estas tierras sagradas de Arco Iris, por sostenerme, por todas sus enseñanzas, la duras y las bellas y por los cuatro vientos, por sus fuerzas que me guían siempre.

Special gratitude *para toda mi familia de sangre o de corazón* who left their city comfort zones to come out to this wild land to help, to visit, to heal, and to support the work here. *Gran abrazo y gracias* to my big brother Jesús and my sisters Diana and Suzanna Moroles for always finding time in your busy lives to love and support me whenever I reached out.

Special gratitude to my great-grandmother Amá Angelita and grandma Antonia, and *todas mis tías*. Special honors to my tía Pepa, auntie Nora Ramirez, and auntie Alma Torres. You were angels in my life, and now you are my Ancestors. Thank you for your unconditional love.

Love and gratitude to *mis primos* Robert, Arturo, and Héctor Ramirez, for always showing up in emergencies, like another set of big brothers. I love you.

Love and gratitude to *mis primas*—Linda and Rosemary Saenz; Silvia, Belinda, and Libby Ramirez; and Lydia Bautista—for all the fun and crazy adventures we had as children, for your continued love and support, and for carrying on as matriarchs of your/our familias after the losses of your mothers. I'm so proud of the strong loving womyn you have become.

My love and deepest appreciation to all my Two-Spirit sisters, who have stood and fought beside me, fighting to protect our Mother, for justice for our people, our children, our culture, and to stay alive. So many of you are my Ancestors now, but memories of you and your strength and *visión* keep me going. To all my beloveds: Marsha Gómez, Patti "Shiner" Cardozo, Bell Keller, Susana Apolonia Santos, Gloria Anzaldúa, Elena Avila, Sheila "Isis" Brown, Burning Cloud, Clary Pérez. Sending out much love and strength to my Two-Spirit hermanas who are still with me and continue to inspire and strengthen me: Mililani Trask, Shylo, Redtail, Celia Herrera Rodríguez, Fann Warren, and so many others making great artistic, social, and spiritual contributions to our communities.

My deepest gratitude to all the Indigenous traditional medicine healers who taught me how to carry the Sacred Bundle of sacred knowledge and universal laws—*curanderas, chamánes, naguales*, Ceremonial and spiritual leaders who taught me what they remembered and also taught me how to remember—and to the many more whom I encountered along this Sacred Red Road. I intentionally sought you out across North, Central, and South America. Thank you for receiving me. It has been a great honor. I remember your teachings and pray they will always live on. José Silva; Ranjana Pallana; Swami Muktananda; Phillip R. Deere and Hokte Deere; Chief Louis Farmer; Chief Leon Shenandoah; George Kingfisher; Effie, Louise, and Jo Ann Yazzie; Janet McCloud; Elena Avila; Julieta Perieda; Enriqueta Conteras; Froilan; Señora Arco Iris Cobb; and Velia Herrera Arredondo—*Tlatzokamati*.

Deepest appreciation to Graciela Sanchez and Gloria Ramirez, editors of *Esperanza* in San Antonio, who, knowing our need and desire to stay informed and connected, have mailed us their newspaper for decades free of charge; to Lee Lanning for her ahead-of-the-times foresight to be inclusive and her contributions to us as marginalized Two-Spirit Womyn of Color on land; and to Julie R., who as editor of *Maize* magazine consciously solicited and featured our work. To Julie Enszer, editor of *Sinister Wisdom*, who also tirelessly solicited me for years to submit writing and featured my work and sent me new books and back issues featuring Womyn of Color for over a decade.

Mil gracias a mis compañeras en esta batalla para apoderar y proteger mujeres, niños, y gente de color y nuestra Tierra Madre. Love you, Marie Cavallo, Lucia Lopez Hall, Lucia Hernández, Virginia Vega, Diana Shiells, Argenis Marín, Francesca García, and Margarita Solorzano.

Much gratitude to my Boxley community, for your consideration, generosity, and the courage to help us when it was not the popular thing to do. Special thanks to Paul and Carol Villines, Norma Lee, Eul Dean, Kathy Carlson, Regina and Bill, Chris and Bryan, Jim and Sandra, Flint and Melissa, Denise Dore, Kerry, Marti, and Thomas and Glenis.

Gracias and *abrazos* to our supporting and ever-growing community: Barbara and Eric, Stacy Wood, Jerry Gene, Francisco, Cheanie and Nick, Karen and Elvin, Alejandro, and Meghan. Much gratitude and strength especially to our Young Bloods: May you keep to this Beauty Way always, Samuel, Taylor, Hiba, Piper, Rebecca, and Zahra—and Parker, our most recent resident steward and my personal health aide and transport. Caring for our Tierra Madre is caring for ourselves and all our Relations.

Much love and appreciation to Diana Rivers for our friendship and her support. *Tlatzokamati* for the big part you played in returning this land to Indigenous womyn and POC stewardship. Eva Kultermann, deepest gratitude for your friendship and loyalty, the work we've done and continue to do together, and our enduring friendship.

Gracias a todos mis pacientes, survivors, and refugees, for trusting me and always generously supporting me, by allowing me to fulfill my life purpose in working with you.

Elise Ashworth, you came to learn, to heal, to grow. You stayed. Now you are a resident steward; now you know the struggles we face. Thank you for the love, respect, caring, and professionalism you bring to the many projects we do together, including this book. Gracias.

With deepest appreciation, I honor the three loves of my life. Thank you for loving and supporting me and allowing me to love you. To love and be truly loved is the greatest blessing of life.

Mil gracias, estimada Dr. Norma Cantú, for your powerful blessing for this book (may the Great Spirit bless you), and to Liliana Wilson, for your soulful artwork and your talent to uplift and give voice to the marginalized with the amazing political art you create. Last, I am grateful to the University of Arkansas Press for the vision and courage to publish this book—that others may find truth, solace, and inspiration to come together for our Mother Earth, for our old and new generations, and for generations to come.

Great Spirit, *Tlatzokamati* for guiding Lauri Umansky to me and this sacred mountain. Lauri, our meeting was not by chance but by Sacred Design. Thank you for having the wisdom and courage to follow your heart and to walk beside me as I retraced my life journey. Writing this book with you has tested us on every level. Thank you for your beauty and grace in walking this often very rocky path with me with so much love, generosity, and patience these past four years. Thank you for making it possible for one Indigenous womoon to share her story with the intention to help others understand our plight, so that together we may help save our beautiful Mother Earth for future generations. Your beauty has won a sacred place in my heart.

Tlatzokamati.

—*María Cristina Moroles / Águila*

ÁGUILA

Prayer for Águila

May the creator be pleased.
May the words written here
reach the ears and eyes of all who need
to hear them. May all who search find
what they need between the covers of this book.
May these nuggets of wisdom feed those
hungry for such knowledge.
Many may be the blessings upon all
who open this book and read these words.
Many may be the tears and the laughter
as those who read or hear these words
are touched, laugh and cry reading.
Imagining and
thinking of the hardship endured,
obstacles overcome,
the many gifts such a life represents,
rejoice!
May this story of a woman like any other, a Tejana,
may this story of a healer, a visionary, a fierce fighter, a survivor,
may it grant solace to those who need it.
May Creator bless the words and help them reach
all who need the messages, the wisdom in these pages.
May Águila soar evermore.
So be it.

—Norma Elía Cantú

1

Awakening

I am an Indigenous woman, a daughter of Tonantzin, my Mother Earth. I am a Two-Spirit Rainbow Prayer Warrior. I am Matriarch of Santuario Arco Iris, a wilderness healing sanctuary in the Ozark Mountains of Arkansas.

A vision led me to this land, with the sacred responsibility to protect my Mother Earth here in all Her aspects—Her water, soil, and rock, and all inhabitants: trees, plants, animals, and all humans. As steward and spiritual leader and teacher, I follow the guidance of nature, my Mother Earth, my Ancestors, and the Ancestors of these lands. Dreams and visions of past, present, and future times guide me.

My Ancestors—Coahuiltecan, Aztec, and Star Nation—lived in our original territories ranging from Utah to southern Texas to the Mexican states of Coahuila and Nuevo León and many parts of the surrounding Mexican states. Turtle Island is my Mother Land.

Like many Indigenous people, we were forcibly displaced from our original homelands. Medicine people and elders from all around our continent have told me the story: We were displaced by white men's wars, their greed, their ignorance. They had lost their true spiritual wisdom, their understanding of universal laws and knowledge.

I first came to this wilderness sanctuary to escape the atrocities of the city that had befallen me. I was led by a vision to this mountain, to heal and protect myself and my daughter. I was led here to live. Initially we sought simply to survive, with the intention to build a place where we could thrive. I needed to reclaim my self-determination, to remember who I truly am.

Over decades, I studied and received wisdom from North and South American masters of their own respected Indigenous teachings and healing practices. My teachers, my community, bestowed upon me, not as badges to flaunt for personal or financial gain, but as recognition of sacred responsibility, these titles: Curandera Total, Chamán, Master Massage Healer, and Águila.

I always remember that I am only a part of a global Indigenous family of women. This memoir documents my story, the herstory of one woman who is similar to millions of Indigenous women. As people of color, as women, we have all struggled and suffered atrocities to survive. This world we live in channels us from birth toward menial service as maids, housekeepers, bodies churning out babies to power the vast farms, factories, and prison systems. The few who hold excessive power live extravagant lifestyles off the backs of people of color and those of low income. They continue to grab our lands, systematically stealing our way of life and denying us the most basic human rights.

I share here my story of waking up to remember our sacredness and the sacred universal laws given to us, the original Indigenous people, by the Creator, telling us to protect our Mother Earth, protect the old, young, poor, and vulnerable.

I pray that my story gives others courage to face the challenges of these crucial, changing times. I share my story to demonstrate that we can rise above our oppressors' theft of positions of power and leadership, of resources, of the very land, our Mother Earth, and all Her bounty.

It is our time as Indigenous women to speak out. We must act NOW for the survival of our Indigenous peoples, our sisters, our children, and our Mother Earth.

I may be labeled a displaced Indigenous woman, but I am not that. My Mother Earth is everywhere I go. She is with me. She led me here. She led me back home to this sacred mountain. She and our Ancestors want us to remember, to never forget, our original ways. They know a time is coming, a time of great Earth changes. Now more than ever, we will need to remember and return to the original ways, to live in harmony with nature and our neighbors, to respect our Mother Earth and Father Sky, to respect ourselves and one another in honorable ways.

What I tell needs to be told. It is the true story, the apple-cider-vinegar version, raw and unfiltered. It takes fortitude to swallow, as it has taken to live. Brace yourself.

I will lead you along the path that brought me to a mountaintop in the Arkansas Ozarks. There my body lay wracked with hepatitis. There I died at the age of twenty-three, as buzzards circled in. On that winter day, as a red-tailed hawk screeched across the brilliant sun, scattering the other birds of prey, I returned to this world as "SunHawk." My new life began.

I am a Two-Spirit Rainbow Prayer Warrior. I am daughter of Tonantzin, my Mother Earth. And make no mistake: I am also a renegade, a rebel, a survivor, a survivalist, an adventurer, a homesteader, and a matriarch. I fear nothing. The Ancestors show the way.

Tlatzokamati (deepest appreciation).

2

Madre

On the twentieth day of December 2017, my mother joined the Ancestors. A *vidente,* a seer, my first teacher of spiritual wisdom, she foresaw my death on the mountain. From afar, she witnessed my rebirth, her Spirit no less present than it had been at my first birth from her own womb. I spoke the eulogy:

How can I honor in words this great woman who was a good daughter, sister, wife, mother, and grandmother? Words can neither encompass nor fully express our Spirit. I will do my best to share with you some few important facts about my mother, María Bautista Moroles, the spiritual matriarch of our family.

She was born in South Texas to a very large, hardworking Indigenous Mexican family. She grew up deeply influenced by two strong spiritual women in her life—her grandmother Amá Angelita (Little Mother Angel) and her mother, Antonia De León Bautista. Mom was a quiet, mostly soft-spoken woman, but when she wanted to be heard, she used few and clear statements. Mom spoke of her mother Antonia always with love, admiration, and gratitude. When she spoke of her grandmother Amá Angelita, she spoke in a tone of awe. Amá Angelita would play the guitar, sing spirituals or songs she made up as they went about their lives. When Mom was young, her family picked cotton to supplement their income. Amá Angelita would often play the guitar and sing to them after a hard day's work.

Dad said that even after Mom married him and birthed baby Jesús, she weighed only 112 pounds. Yet, he would brag, she could pick more cotton than anyone else in the whole crew. She would drag her sack of cotton down the long rows in the hot sun, with baby Jesús lying atop the sack as she picked her cotton.

When Mom was young, she lived in a town named Robstown, Texas, later declared a Superfund site, where the highest levels of toxic waste were dumped. She suffered her whole life with various autoimmune disorders I believe to have been caused by exposure to toxic chemicals, there and as a farm worker. I often called Mom the bionic woman because she had so many operations and artificial joints. Yet she rarely complained. She enjoyed her life.

María Bautista Moroles was a stoic woman who always put family first in her life. She gave birth to six children, three girls and three boys, in this order: Jesús, Joe Jr., María Cristina, Diane, Hilario "Lalo," and Suzanna. Mom's sisters, with their contagious laughter and love, were her best friends: my tías, Alma, Josie, Mena, Nora, and Sulema. My dad José was the love of her life, her pledge for sixty-eight years. Her children were her life and her pride. Mom's spiritual beliefs and practices were her Staff of Life.

I will always remember Mom making beans, arroz con pollo, salsa, and big stacks of fresh homemade corn tortillas every day. When we were kids, she worked across town for rich families, cleaning, cooking, and caring for their children. She had to ride two buses to get to work and two back. Though I'm sure she was very tired, she still came home and took care of us. She would come to see that we were all there and then go straight into the kitchen to cook for us. Mom always made sure we were ready for school. Boy, do I remember getting my hair braided before school, the strands pulled back so tight that my eyes rose an inch; with three girls, it had to be done quickly. Mom always made sure we were bathed and well fed. Our clothes, rarely new, were always clean.

Although we were considered poor, Mom was generous. Right away, she found something to feed those who came to visit: a cup of coffee, an egg, beans or papitas—and, always, fresh tortillas. When we traveled to Mexico to visit family, Mom would pack useful clothing in extra suitcases to leave with the needy families we visited every year. Now I wonder how she could pack for all eight of us and still get those extra suitcases on our station wagon. I know it was a miracle.

Mom went from cleaning others' houses for meager pay to visiting the White House as an honored guest. She dined with the rich and famous and attended fine functions when her son Jesús received the National Medal of Arts in 2008. President George W. Bush praised "his enduring achievements as a sculptor of stone." While she was quiet and sometimes felt out of place, Mom carried herself proudly and graciously in all circles, rich or poor.

There was a very special side to my mother that she shared with no one but me. Now that she has gone on from this world, I feel it is important for me to tell this. My mother had a gift. In Spanish she would be called *una vidente*—a seer, a clairvoyant. I think her gift was a burden to her. She kept it secret, never wanting to trouble others. When I was in my early twenties, Mom began to share her special dreams and visions with me. She knew intuitively that I would understand. These dreams or visions or premonitions mostly foretold tragedies to come. I know they helped to prepare her for what was to come. Her gift gave her wisdom beyond her age and helped her guide her family through the many difficult times we were to face in this life.

I left my mountain home to be with my dying mom. I heard her call before I became consciously aware of her impending departure from this reality we call life. Mom is now with the Ancestors. We feel a deep loss. But someday soon we will meet again. Together we will walk in beauty once more.

Tlatzokamati.

3

Dallas: House

We lived in the projects for the first two years after Dad led the family migration to Dallas from Corpus Christi, Texas, in the mid-1950s. They were mixed projects in Dallas, all poor people, Black, white, Indian, and Latino. Faded red brick as far as the eye could see. Dad wanted desperately to move us out of there, where shootings and stabbings occurred with regularity. Drunkenness and discord spilled into the street and onto our doorstep. Police sirens formed the natural sounds of the night. He wanted to get us out. That was his vision and goal.

Eventually, with my father's help, almost all of our extended family left Corpus, where there was no work and no food, to move north. Only my great-grandmother Amá Angelita and a couple of her children stayed behind. I remember visiting her tiny unpainted house with a picket fence— the little pointy wooden boundary just feet from her door. The small yard teemed with people. She had called in *la familia* for her final hours.

Everyone exclaimed, "María and José! You got here! They're here!" We were the last to arrive. We went in and stood around her bed. I was four years old. I wiggled my way to her bedside, standing at her level, peering into her face. Her gray eyes moved slowly from face to face to face, seeing that all had come. She smiled at me, then put her head back down, just like that.

That is the way it should be. You should be able to decide.

*/ */ */

I recall the gaze of my parents. I was the third child born to them. Mom
cried after birthing two boys. She wanted a daughter. Dad also prayed
for a girl. They named me María Cristina, after the blessed Mother Mary,
Mother of Christ. Being the first boy in the family, Jesús had been like
Christ himself. And Joe had arrived in between.

As nicknames took hold within the family, they often called me *la guera*,
the fair-skinned one. More often, they laughingly recalled that I had been
named after a song, "María Cristina Me Quiere Gobernar," which spoke of
a young woman who was very bossy with her boyfriend and how he always
complied. It is true that Jesús and I, as their oldest boy and girl, as in all
traditional Indigenous families, acted as parents in Mom and Dad's absence.
We held more responsibility than the other children. I'm sure the young
ones found me bossy.

*/ */ */

When I turned four, I went to a daycare at the YMCA in downtown Dallas.
I looked forward to that bus ride with Mom downtown. She would catch
another bus to work after she dropped me off.

As soon as you entered the YMCA, a woman would take all your clothes
off you and fold them neatly into a basket with a number on it. Then she
would dress you in a little jumper with the same number on it. With so
many kids in that giant basement of the Y, they did not try to learn our
names. I did not speak there. They did not understand my words.

The noise of many children corralled from place to place, some understanding the language spoken and some not, intrigued me. I smelled the
chlorine from the pool, felt the steamy warmth of the place. I waited for
the old Mexican lady who put us through the showers at the end of the
day. She would dry me off and dress me in the clothes from my little num-
bered basket. As she combed my hair, making me all spick-and-span for
my mother to pick me up, she spoke to me in my language. She knew my
name. She knew my words.

*/ */ */

The next year, our family moved up the hill to La Loma, a little bit out of the projects, still in West Dallas. It was the ugliest old house you could imagine. It had no plumbing, only an outhouse. All around lay white limestone. No grass, no dirt. Nothing. The house stood all by itself, high up on stilts, next to an old limestone quarry. Other houses, beyond, had been fixed up.

Dad said, "We can fix this up."

He did that, as the babies kept coming. That was all he did. He went to work, he came home, he worked on that house, our limestone quarry palace. He put in plumbing and rewired the electricity throughout. He built an indoor bathroom and a laundry room. Each of the four rooms had its purpose. Mom ruled the kitchen, where the radio, always on, played ranchero music as she prepared the food of her own childhood. She and Dad slept in the living room. Once the full roster of children had arrived, we slept three girls in one bedroom, three boys in the other.

Dad took pride in the brand-new siding he bought at the unclaimed salvage yard and affixed to the house himself. Each facade had a different kind of siding. Each looked good, as long as you didn't turn the corner or remember the last side you had viewed.

In Corpus, Dad had washed windows. He had taken any work he could find. Then he married into the sprawling Bautista family, joining them as migrant labor in the fields. He fared poorly there, with no upward path visible. This did not suit him. José Moroles had ambition. Wherever he stood, he sought the next rung, and the next.

From the age of three, when his father died of liver failure, he had known the pangs of an empty belly. The scant earnings of a widow could not stretch far enough to feed many mouths, and the church offered only prayers. He had crossed the border alone at the age of eleven, from Monterrey, in search of his older brother, *Tío* Santos. In all, he crossed the border undocumented twenty-seven times. He was captured and returned to Mexico twenty-seven times, and twenty-seven times he swam the Rio Grande to return to the United States. There would be food on his family's table and clothes on his children's backs as long as he had breath.

He found a job at an optical place in Corpus, where Dr. Pearle hired him as a cleanup guy. Right away, Dad noticed another Mexican man there actually grinding the lenses. "Teach me how," he asked the man, Ruben Arroyo, who over time became Dad's close friend. "I will come early. I will stay late. Teach me." He learned quickly. Before long, Dr. Pearle took notice. He promoted "Joe" Moroles first to lens grinding, and then over many years, in Dallas, into supervisory positions in his growing optical empire.

Once when Dad went to Mexico to visit his mother and his sister, he got stopped at the border without papers. Dr. Pearle intervened: "No, you're not taking him. He works for me." When appendicitis struck, Mom called Dr. Pearle: "I don't know what to do." Dr. Pearle came over, lifted Dad into his own car, drove him to the hospital where his physician performed the surgery, and paid the bill. Mrs. Pearle brought us clothing that her three children outgrew. Dr. Pearle would ask my dad to take his kids fishing. Dad was happy to do it; we all went to the lake in the projects. Dr. Pearle sent Dad to night school for vocational business training.

Dr. Pearle eventually went into business with two other men whose management practices squeezed the workers. Dad, a supervisor at the time, led the workers out on a picket line. He got fired. "Nothing I can do about this, Joe," Dr. Pearle told him. "I'm in business with these men. But I'm getting out." When Dr. Pearle went back on his own, Dad started working with him again.

They helped each other in ways each understood. They loved each other.

When I was six years old, Dad gave me a gift, a gift of words, a gift from the Ancestors. He took me aside and spoke solemnly. "You are getting ready to go to school. They are going to lie to you about a lot of things. They might treat you differently. But you always remember that you are proud. You are proud first because you are an Indian; second, because you are a Mexican; and last, because you are an American. They are going to say things to you. Do not ever believe them."

It was a mixed school of poor kids—poor whites, poor Blacks, and poor Latinos—staffed with teachers who could not get jobs in the "better" schools. All white teachers. I did not speak English. Many of us did not. They told us we could not speak Spanish, that we would be punished if we did. A little Mexican girl with black, glossy hair plaited neatly, forbidden to speak her needs, stood beside me in line with pee dripping down her legs on the first day of school.

"If you speak Spanish, you will be punished." The teachers demonstrated their resolve. Speak Spanish, get put in the hall. Speak Spanish, get spanked. Some teachers were downright mean. My parents had never raised a hand to me.

The first year, the school let us bring our lunches. Mom prepared them last thing before she went to bed at night, leaving foil-wrapped packages tucked into paper bags for each of us school-aged children. I opened mine eagerly at lunchtime, inhaling the home scents of beans and meat wrapped in a homemade tortilla. Mom sent two tacos each day, and a piece of fruit.

Then the school authorities decided that for us to be integrated into society, we could not eat our traditional foods. Any student who ate that kind of food needed tokens to buy the school lunch from the cafeteria. They started giving us tokens.

A little white girl named Darlene sat beside me in class. We had both tested into the "smarter" group. She saw my confusion about the items on the lunchroom tray—the slab of meat, the fork and knife. At my house, we used tortillas and a spoon. Mom would cut all the meat and put it in the tortilla. Or if she made chicken wings, we just used our hands. Darlene demonstrated how to use the utensils. I watched and learned. Their food tasted like wood. It had no aroma.

They accused us of stealing things, stealing all the time. Food. Paper. Chalk. Loose change. Books. White kids' stuff. Always, they singled out the Latino and Black kids. I was not afraid of them. I did not steal. I would not admit to something I had not done. I would not make false confession. I would not name others, either. They could and did paddle me. I would never cry. My show of indifference infuriated them.

By second grade, I began to seethe. I became an angry little girl, always taking up for the kids who were not prepared as I had been prepared. I felt privileged. My dad had told me what was in store. I would tell my brown and Black classmates, "They are lying! Don't believe them! Be proud!"

My mother lamented the change. "How can this be?" she would say. "I sent an angel to school and I got back an angry little devil!"

In the second grade, Jerry Melton, a white boy, got a crush on me. He chased me everywhere. One day he pulled my braids all the way down the jungle gym. I pursued him back into the school building. As I grabbed him, he fell down the concrete stairs and broke his arm. Breaking a little white boy's arm was a serious offense. They tried to expel me for that one.

My parents came to the school. Mom was a humble woman. She would not look at them. She would hardly speak. But Dad, who knew English pretty well, wanted the full story. He stood up to the principal and demanded to know.

"She pushed him. End of story," the principal said. "Didn't you?"

"Yes." I was not going to lie.

"Why did you push him?" Dad asked. When the full story came out, they could not simply expel me.

That is how it would go. Dad would act irate with the white authority, get me back in school, talk to me about right and wrong, and let it go. My report cards came home with all *A*'s and a bunch of *X*'s in conduct and self-control. Same with my brother Joe. Jesús, the eldest, played it real straightlaced, always out to please. He excelled in academics and art and sports. Joe and I were the only troublemakers.

If anyone had asked me why I kept getting in trouble, I would have told them: I did not want to be mistreated. I would not confess to something I had not done just because they wanted more reason to punish me. I knew they wanted to break me, and I was not going to let them. I was an Indian. I was a Mexican. I was an American. And I was one more thing, too: I was a human being. I was proud. I wanted to be treated fairly. Outrage boiled up inside me.

At home, we did not talk about school. We came home and did our chores. Jesús and I watched the younger children—Diane, Lalo, and Suzanna, the baby. We did our homework on an honor system. Our parents never checked it. They could not have helped us with it anyway. If we finished it in time, we could watch one TV show, usually Disney or *The Twilight Zone* or Hitchcock.

Every spare minute, we all worked on the homestead. Under Dad's direction, we landscaped our rock-quarry yard with lush grass surrounded by rose bushes. We had two horses, which I tended, and many chickens. We had a sanctuary, built with our own labor from found items, other people's leftovers. Dad taught us to envision beauty and to work to make it.

Work and exhaustion crowded out talk. We did not discuss politics in the house, only bills and the needs of us kids. Even religion got short-changed. Dad, who had grown up Catholic, had no patience for the church. Where had it been when his widowed mother struggled to feed her children? When a Baptist church in our neighborhood started recruiting us, as her own mother had been recruited and converted years earlier, Mom made some effort to bring us to Sunday services, but she did not need a church to ignite her spirituality. Plus, she was bone-tired.

Mom's body showed her exhaustion long before she had the privilege to work less, or even to sit down in the course of a day's work. She developed rheumatoid arthritis in her late twenties. During her pregnancy with Suzanna, when I was perhaps nine years old, varicose veins mangled her legs. I would see her struggling down the drive to our house in the evening, her ankles bulging, her breath labored, as we ran out to greet her.

To me she said, "Go under the house to gather cobwebs. If I ever get cut, or if these veins burst, run to get the cobwebs. We will put them on my cut, as Amá Angelita taught me."

I collected cobwebs for Mom's legs. They soothed her. And I began to wonder why my beautiful mother had to stand all day on legs deformed by overuse while cooking, cleaning, and caring for another woman's children. I thought long and hard on that question.

Ah, but we had weekends, free from school and work and other people's families. Weekends brought the Moroles, Bautista, Ramirez, Saenz, Torres, and Lopez families together—tías and tíos and scores of children. We did not need outside friends; we had cousins. Most lived in La Loma, close by. We could run from one house to another. When we got hungry, a tía fed us. Five or six kids would push the lawnmower up and down the neighborhood until we earned enough money to get us all into the Mexican movie matinee. Often, we invented games, like running barefoot on the melting tar roads, testing who had the thickest soles or greatest endurance.

In warm weather, we might go to the lake, piling into each other's cars, always at least twenty kids in tow. Or we would head out to the flatlands and wild pecan groves, where the Dallas Fort Worth International Airport now stands, to gather pecans, visit, and picnic together.

Many times, we gathered in the backyard of one of my tías or tíos in La Loma for a pig kill. The men would slaughter the giant pig and butcher it all up, as the kids looked on in some horror. Then the women would take over, making use of every bit of meat and fat they could salvage from the creature. They would fry the fat for oil, chop the meat for tamales, raid the innards for chitterlings. Everyone went home with food.

My father made delicacies from the slaughterhouses' refuse: cow heads. They sold them cheap to the Mexicans. Dad had a deep pit in our backyard, specifically for cooking cow heads. He would buy two of them each time. On Saturday nights, the men of the family would sit around the fire pit getting the coals ready. The women gathered in the house, talking, laughing, and wrapping the cow heads, layer over layer, with oiled paper bags, the many layers forming an encasement that obscured the shape of the heads. Dad would throw these mummies onto a grate in the pit, cover that with tin, and lay fire on top. The men sat out there as the meat smoked. Their voices carried into the house, where the women also sang and told stories, which they interrupted occasionally to bring food and coffee out to the men, until finally, many hours later, the fire went out.

Then on Sunday mornings, they would all come back. The women inside prepared sopa, tortillas, salsa, beans, and rice as the men lifted the wrapped heads from the pit and stripped the meat away. The cheeks had a lot of meat, as did the tongue. Everything came out: the brains, the eyes. They would separate it all on big dishes for the women to use.

In the meantime, the older kids would cross over the wall separating our yard from a big fenced-in area below. We had crafted this wall—which ran about one hundred feet long and four feet high—from cement blocks Dad had recycled from building sites. There, our two horses roamed free, without saddles, officially unbroken. We took turns riding them as long as we could last, grabbing their manes as they ran and bucked, until we slid off into the grass. Our parents sat up in our yard watching the entertainment, cheering us on every now and then. I loved those wild horses, and I loved those long Sundays when Dallas felt like paradise and Monday felt far away.

Come Monday, back to the grind. I lurched through Sidney Lanier Elementary School, spending many hours sitting outside the principal's office. Occasionally I had a kind teacher, like Miss McCowan in sixth grade. By then I was tall and twiggy, reed-thin. The boys liked me in the strange way of boys that age. They loved to grab my braids, which got me fighting in the dirt with them, and winning. Miss McCowan would talk to me about it.

Not the other teachers. I got into it one day with the music teacher. I got so mad that I knocked my desk over. She came over and pinched me in the side with her long nails, a deep gouge. When Dad came up to the school to get me, I lifted my shirt to show him the wound. "You do not do this to my child," he told the woman. "If she does something wrong, you call me. You do NOT do this to my child." They expelled me anyway.

Miss Marks, my sixth-grade art teacher, troubled me in a different way. Her blue eyes and dark hair distracted me, especially when she wore a particular red A-line dress. I wanted her attention, any attention—good, bad, racist, *any crumb*. I spent most of her class in the hall on punishment.

One day, at the end of the school year, when she was paying me no mind, I snapped a pen in two, snaking blue ink across her chair. As she sat, the wetness creeping through her tight red dress, her eyes flashed toward me. She screamed for her buddy, Miss Green in the next classroom over, who dragged me out to the hall and flung me up against the lockers. Miss Marks followed, shouting, "Didn't she tell you to face that locker?" As I turned toward the locker, she took my head in her hands and banged it, once, twice, three times against the metal.

When elementary school ended, things got rougher. Dallas integrated its schools, with city buses carrying poor kids of all races along many routes.

Jesús ended up going to Crozier Tech, a high school geared toward trades. He continued along as he always had, unbothered and excellent at everything he touched: academics, sports, art. He hung his first art show in the sixth grade, selling pieces for five or ten cents each in the very halls where I sat out much of elementary school on discipline. Success lapped at Jesús from the start.

In 1965, Joe and I got sent to Pinkston High in West Dallas, an all-Black high school recently mandated to integrate racially. It also had to accommodate junior high school kids because construction on the new middle school building lagged. Swollen with too many kids, ranging from puny seventh graders to massive twelfth graders, Pinkston exploded early into violence.

Fights—bad fights—erupted daily. If the Black kids defended their turf at first, soon enough the Latinos got together, the whites got together, and it was on. Beatings, stabbings, murder. Doors chained shut. Armed cops policing the halls.

I stood in the hallway when a boy I knew, a friend, staggered out of the bathroom, stabbed in the chest. He dropped right there and died.

I did not get through a week without being beaten up. That is what going to school meant. Getting your nose broken or your lip bloodied. Getting bruised up. I would always clean myself up and try to look presentable. Sometimes on the way home I would stop to see my father's cousin's wife, Socorro. She and her husband were from Mexico; Dad had helped them cross the border. Even when I was in elementary school, after I'd get in fights, I would stop at her house. She'd say, "What have you been doing?" She would redo my hair, fix me up, and get me back out there.

I guess I cleaned up enough for my parents not to notice. Plus, they had six children. Lalo, who was born with a heart defect, required constant attention. He needed expensive medication. He could not be made to get excited. I brought home a straight-A report card. I brought home a paycheck from my after-school cashiering job at the local drugstore. I did not want to bring home trouble, and they did not ask about school.

Over the summer before seventh grade, during swim class at the YMCA, I got stomach cramps. A girl in my group led me to the bathroom, where she put a nickel into a machine to buy a pad. "You put it on and you bleed on that," she explained. "Girls all start that. It happens every month for a few days. No swimming while you are bleeding!" I mentioned the blood to my mother only because I would need nickels for the machine. She said nothing, only nodded, and then a package of pads appeared in my room. We did not talk about our bodies in my home. We did not reveal our bodies in my home. I never saw my parents less than fully clothed.

At Pinkston, I learned to play hooky from classes when the chaos overwhelmed me. There was a technique. You would slip into the bathroom unseen just as a class period began, then lock the stall door for a few minutes of solitude. If someone entered the bathroom, you lifted your feet to remain unseen.

I was doing that one afternoon, doubled over with cramps, with a friend in the neighboring stall. I thought I had locked my door. An older student, one of the bathroom monitors who came to bust smokers and class skippers, plowed through kicking stall doors and cussing. I didn't have time to put my feet up. She saw them and whammed the door into my face. "Get the fuck out of there! You should be in class!" She yanked me from the stall and beat the crap out of me, even as I cussed her out the whole while. Big old eleventh grader. When she left, my girlfriend came out of her stall to clean me up for the next class period.

I must have looked a little bruised when I got home that day, but I guess no one noticed. I felt relieved not to be questioned. My parents had enough problems. I did not want to create more for them.

A Mexican girl working at the drugstore started talking to me. I felt flattered that Lucia, a sophomore at Pinkston, would actually speak to a mere seventh grader like me. "Come over to my house and watch TV tomorrow," she said. "The school doesn't notice if you skip."

I hesitated. Ditching an entire day seemed of a different magnitude than hiding out for a class period here and there. Then again, a day's vacation from Hell appealed to me. We set it up. Her parents would be at work. We would have the house to ourselves. I might as well try it.

I had been there a while when a boy showed up, also Latino and a sophomore at Pinkston High. Lucia left to grab something from the store. She waved lightly, "I'll be back."

Gabriel lit a cigarette, sending a little round smoke puff in my direction.

It happened quickly. He pinned me on the couch. I had never been kissed or held hands or gone on a date. I was twelve years old.

"You wanted me," he said. "You wanted that. If you talk about it, I will tell the whole school about you. Slut. Whore. *Puta.*"

I do not remember leaving Lucia's house or getting home or whether it was warm or cold on that day. I felt sticky with blood, terrified that my parents would know I had skipped school. Gutted. Flayed. Embarrassed. The shame went too deep to fathom. I had skipped school; I had caused this to happen. I washed and washed and washed myself, and I did not speak of what had happened.

I would see Gabriel in the hall at school. I would see Lucia. They both avoided me. I left the job at the drugstore to join my cousin at a waitressing job at Chubby's instead. I pressed on. I would come home late from work, around the same time as Dad. Nothing changed, except that sometimes a sharp sense of dread clutched my breath and my sight went blurry.

✒ ✒ ✒

A few months later, my mother confronted me. I was the only one using the pads. "I haven't seen that you're using any," she said.

"I don't need to. I haven't needed them."

She looked hard at me. Then she slapped me. There was nothing said after that.

The next day, she took me to the doctor. Pregnant, he said. Too late for an abortion, which was not legal in Texas in 1965 anyway.

Mom apparently told Dad that day. He would not look at me. He would not talk to me. I had been an esteemed daughter who helped the family, even worked and brought in some money. Now, I brought shame upon the Moroles name.

They decided to bring me to Rockport, where my father's older sister lived. We drove through the night in complete silence as I tried to recall my tía's husband's name. Julian. Julian and Josefina Tapia. Tía Fina. Tío Tapia. They were well into their thirties, maybe older, with no children. They worked together as masons, hard labor with artisanal beauty. But they were not joyful people.

"We will adopt this baby," Tía Fina told me. "And you will go to school here, in your shame." *Embarazada*, the Spanish word for pregnant, hit me as my belly rammed forward from my tight hips and I pushed through classes in a sweltering, overcrowded school, talking to no girls, no boys, no adults. On weekends, I did masonry with Tía Fina and Tío Tapia, lifting blocks, carrying supplies.

"You got what you deserved," my tía would say. "Shame, shame, shame." While I did not dispute that, I began to feel a tiny flicker of rage, the slightest rekindling of the angry girl who had knocked over desks and fought boys in the schoolyard. Why had no one, not one single person, asked me how I got pregnant? If they did ask, I decided, I would not tell them. I would give away nothing. *Nada.* Never again.

From my room, I heard my tía on the phone telling my mother to come to Rockport. "Her time is soon."

No one prepared me for labor. I knew where the baby had to come out; I just did not know how. When the pains started, I determined to make no sound. A whimper escaped. I heard my tío waking my tía, "I think you need to take her to the clinic."

I lay alone in the dingy walk-in clinic, staffed entirely by white people. Sometimes the doctor or nurse would come in: "Lay still!" "Shut up!" "It's supposed to hurt!" "We'll tie your hands back if you don't keep them still." "Be quiet!" Loud voices. White faces. Finally, they yelled "push! push!" For what seemed like hours, I tried to push the baby out. It would not budge.

I prayed silently for the baby to come out before my mother arrived. More than anything, I dreaded the shame of her witnessing the birth.

Then came forceps, wrangling and tugging inside me. The nurse pushed my legs open wider, as the doctor dug for the baby. "This one's stubborn," he said. I felt a powerful yank and heard him say, "It's a boy."

My tía came in after a while, holding a beautiful baby boy—dark eyes, black hair, a tightly swaddled bundle. "His name is Julian," she said. "After his father." I signed adoption papers.

The clinic sent me back to my tía's house that morning. By evening, my mother had arrived. We boarded a Greyhound bus for Dallas that very night. For twelve hours, as the bus stopped at every dusty corner of Texas, I curled up inside my coat. My hips felt jagged at the joints. My breasts, bound tight, pounded and filled. I felt hollowed out, too weak to tell Mom that I might not be able to walk off the bus in Dallas. At some point, she covered me with a blanket. As the outskirts of the city came into view, she broke the silence of the trip with three words: "Don't tell anyone."

Baby Julian looked normal in the photographs. We did not know until many months later that he had been damaged by the forceps. He started having problems, delays at each point of development: walking, talking, and all that came after. He developed epileptic-type seizures.

Tío Tapia died when Julian Jr. turned ten. Tía Fina would hiss at me whenever she saw me at family gatherings, usually funerals, "You are cursed! You ruined my baby!"

4

Dallas: Street

Little Suzanna flew into my arms as I entered the house. "María Cristina! My María Cristina! Where have you been?" She had been like my baby. My whole body ached. Her little hands reached out, grabbing for me. I pulled away. No part of me was up for this now. Everything had changed. I had changed. Mom and Dad barely spoke to me.

Some days later, I heard the mailman outside. Bringing in the mail had always been my chore. As habit, I went out to fetch it. Bills. A letter from Tía Fina addressed to my father. An official-looking government envelope addressed to me.

I hid it in my pocket until I could be alone. In the bathroom, I opened the envelope quietly. I felt it had to be something important. I was right: an income tax refund check for $125! I had no idea the government did that. I knew not to mention it, though my mind reeled with ideas. I would give myself time to think. What could I do with this money? I knew I had to go away.

Tension filled the house. Dad would not speak to me. Mom said very little. He yelled at her now, finding fault with her for wrinkles in his work shirt, too little salt in the arroz con pollo. She said nothing. I listened from my room, where Suzanna, then three, snuggled up to me during these storms.

One day, hardly thinking, I dashed out to the kitchen during one of his tirades. "When I get married," I yelled, "I'll never marry somebody like you!" The words came from somewhere.

He looked at me, his eyes wild. Quietly, deliberately, he said, "Nobody will ever marry you."

I was done. I knew my parents to be people of few words, never anything brutal. That was all he said. I was done with them.

From my bedroom, I grabbed a small purse. Into it I stuffed my Social Security card and the refund check. Nothing else. I took no clothes, nothing. He had spoken those words to me, and I was done.

I took the check to the grocery store where I used to help my parents cash their checks and pay their bills. Every English-speaking child of immigrants knows how to do that. I went right up to the storekeeper and handed him my check and Social Security card. That's all I had. He cashed my check, taking his fee. No questions, no words.

$$\mathscr{F} \; \mathscr{F} \; \mathscr{F}$$

At the downtown bus station, I bought a one-way ticket to Tampa, Florida, the furthest place I could go with a little money left over. I figured I could get by until I got a job. I was thirteen.

The bus trip from Dallas to Tampa took three days, with stops at every hole-in-the-wall town along the Gulf Coast. My seat mates changed frequently. I spoke to none of them. I bought chips and candy at the quick stops. At a long stop, I spotted a hamburger joint next door. I still remember that burger, thin and soggy as it was. Water came free from the fountain at most stops. I got by.

At the bus station in Tampa, I set my little purse on the sink counter as I splashed cool water on my face for the first time in three days. Then I slipped into a bathroom stall for a minute. Upon emerging, I remembered that I had left my purse on the counter. Gone. I had absolutely nothing but the clothes on my back.

As the bus depot door swung closed behind me, I felt no fear, no remorse. I knew what I was doing. I was leaving for good, never to go back. I was done. I had been a good daughter. They had taught me everything I needed to know. My girl cousins and I had sold our home-baked cupcakes door-to-door for money to go to the Mexican theater matinee in our neighborhood. I had mowed yards, sold pop bottles for a few cents apiece, and had already earned paychecks for a year. Dad had taken us fishing. He taught us how to shoot a rifle. By eleven, I could drive our station wagon. I could ride a horse. My parents had taught me how to work, how to survive. I knew I could get by. I felt no fear. I was done.

♪♪♪

The warm, briny air drew me to the beach, which I reached quickly on foot, running the last block to the sand, where I kicked off my shoes, rolled up my pant legs, and dashed into the water. Wading out into its expanse, I felt free as the waves lapped around me and the sun licked my bare shoulders. I might have stood there a short while or a long while. I am not sure.

I went to sit in the sand where I had dropped my shoes. I sat for several hours, as the high sun began to dip toward the west. A few yards away, a white family of two parents and two young children picnicked and played all afternoon beneath an umbrella. Eventually, the lady came over to me, sweat dripping from her bleached bouffant. "You want a sandwich?" she asked. "Where's your parents?"

"My parents aren't here. I'm by myself."

"Oh, well, you want to join us?" They fed me and gave me some Kool-Aid. "You're getting too much sun. It's awful hot out here. Are you sure you shouldn't call your parents and go home?"

"I'm on my own."

"How old are you?"

"Eighteen."

She rolled her eyes. "Well, you're burnt as bacon. That's not good for you and you have not been drinking water. Where are you going tonight?"

"I'm not sure yet."

She looked toward her husband, who nodded. "Why don't you come over to our house? We'll get some food and water in you."

At least I didn't puke in their station wagon. I remember icy sheets on hot skin, and heaving into a bucket, as the woman came in and out of the darkened room to place cloths on my forehead. Voices drifted in. "She can't be much more than fifteen." "Mommy, can she stay here?" A night and a day passed, maybe twice that. My shoulders blistered from the sunburn; my face peeled.

Three or four days later, vitality returned. I soaked in a deep bath capped with clouds of lilac-scented bubbles. Later I joined the two blond-haired children at their backyard picnic table for grilled cheese sandwiches cut into triangles. I began to plan my departure.

Then a uniformed policeman appeared in the doorway.

"I'm sorry," the mother said. "We are very worried about you. I'm sure your family is too. We had to call the police."

The police questioned me at the station, good cop, bad cop style. I would not speak. Even if my parents had called the police and put out an all-points bulletin, what was the likelihood they could identify me? Thousands of kids ran away each year.

Soon, however, I sat next to a stern policewoman on a plane back to Dallas, where the authorities took me into custody and brought me to a juvenile detention center.

Again, I sat silent through a crisp interrogation.

The juvenile detention lady finally said, "We know who you are. I have your picture." She showed it to me. "Your parents are looking for you, María. They're going to come over here this afternoon. To pick you up."

"I'm not going. I'm not going anywhere. I'm not going with them." That was the only time I would speak.

They did not make me see or speak to my parents after all that day. Instead, at an emergency hearing, the juvenile court judge ordered me into foster care as soon as a placement could be found.

At juvie that night, a Black girl hanged herself in the bathroom. Another girl, who made guttural noises, no words, lumbered around the room where eight of us were supposed to be sleeping, leaning her massive body over to peer directly into our faces. She was in for stealing mail, someone said.

I had to get out of that room. In the morning, I surveyed the scene, picked my mark, and made my move. Tink, the smallest girl called herself. She was a "habitual runaway" with long blond hair and a hopeful smile. I shoved her against the wall and got up in her face for a fight.

The staff charged in. "Break it up! Break it up!"

Solitary was a whole lot better, except for the caseworker who insisted that I talk to her. I didn't have anything I wanted to tell her. Weeks passed. Finally, one day, she said, "You're going into a foster home."

🪶 🪶 🪶

Some perverse devil must have been making the foster-care placements that week. In walked my mother's preacher, *Hermano* Maestas, and his wife. He was Mexican, the wife white. I had last seen him days after I returned home from Rockport, still weak from giving birth. My mother asked him to baptize me. He spoke to her, not me. "I cannot do that, Señora Moroles. She has been pregnant out of wedlock. She is unclean."

Now he took me to live with him and his wife and his two kids in an Ozzie and Harriet suburb of Dallas. They took me shopping for all these stupid plaid clothes and made a show of praying before they did every goddamn thing. I barely spoke to them during the short time I stayed there, all the while planning my escape. I would not live under anyone's rule ever again.

The court also required me to see a counselor. *Hermana* Maestas drove me there each week, to a small brick building in the city, where the perfectly nice counselor would talk and talk and talk to me as I stared through her, wondering whether I'd launch a more successful getaway from there, or from the Maestas house, or from the godless church they dragged my unclean soul to each Sunday. I would never talk to her.

After weeks of counseling, the nice counselor, whose name was Deborah, said, "You're going to have to talk to me, because if you don't, they're going to give you shock therapy." Tears welled in her eyes. "Please just say something to me, anything, so I can report that you spoke, that we're making some progress. Because you do not want to get shock therapy. It's very terrible."

She talked me into it. I spoke to her a little bit. I didn't tell her much. She asked how I felt. "I don't feel," I told her.

After a couple of weeks, she said, "Your parents are going to come next week to our session. I will be here the whole time. I will be here for you." I had not seen them since I left home.

Anger bolted through me. I recalled my resolve to never trust them again. Yet I felt a sense of terror that I could not put into words. The room seemed to shrink. I began to sweat and to shake. A dank, heavy dread started building within me, rising and rising, until I could not breathe.

Deborah spoke calmly to me, "Take a slow breath in, María. And let it out. You are safe. It is okay." We sat for a while.

On the morning of the meeting with my parents, Hermana Maestas told me I could stay home from school. She wanted to braid my hair to look pretty for my mother, who would be so happy to see me. I would not let her touch me.

The room began to spin as Hermana Maestas spoke, her voice growing dimmer and dimmer. My breath came fast, too fast to catch, like an explosion from within, and I shook, wracked with involuntary motion, as a voice rose from within me, a voice without words, a scream so forceful and essential that it must have made sound, but I could not hear it. I covered my ears and rolled up into a ball. Something broke inside.

🖋 🖋 🖋

"Nervous breakdown," the attendant at Parkland Hospital declared as they transferred me from the ambulance to a gurney, then strapped me down and rolled me through halls, long white lights passing overhead, muted voices all around. I could not move. I could not shield myself. I decided never to feel again.

In a small bright room they shot me up with Thorazine.

Deborah came to see me. She stroked my hand and guided my breathing. "Long breath in, María. And let it flow out. Long breath in." A young nurse came in to take my vital signs. Then a doctor, with a needle. "More Thorazine," he said. "The good stuff." The nurse giggled.

Deborah sat with me, holding my hand. I thought for a moment that she was my mother, younger and paler and plainer. No, she could not be my mother. Mom had to work. Is it day or night? Where are my clothes? Why am I in a hospital gown? My God, where are my underclothes? Where? Restraints hold me. Don't look, Mamá; I will cover this. I try to search in the sheets, clawing, but my wrists are strapped. The white doctor pushes me down. I see bars on the window. I am exposed. Cigarette mouth. Is this real? Ripped. Torn apart. His hot breath, sour, holding me down. Words in my face: *Puta*. Slut. You want this. You wanted me. Don't say anything. You'll be sorry. I buck like my unbroken horse. I throw him. Sound forms in my depths and works through my lips as word: No, no, no, no, NO. NO. NO. NO. Get away from me.

For a long while, Deborah held my hand. She stroked my head. I tasted my own tears for the first time I could remember. I saw her tears. We breathed. I began to drift.

When I woke, she was still there. "Now we know," she said. "Now you can begin to heal."

She met with my parents and told them all. She did not advise visitation at that time.

They kept me there for a while, in the psych ward. Deborah came to see me each day. She helped me.

Finally, one day she came in and said, "Your parents want to see you. They feel badly. They really need to see you. Can you let them come in? You don't have to say anything. I'll stay with you," she said.

She did stay. They came in. Mom wept and held me. Dad paced the small room, head down, repeating over and over, "I am sorry. I am so sorry." That's all I remember.

A few weeks later, Deborah asked me if I wanted to go back home. I said I never wanted to go back home. I was done with that life.

The court placed me with my tía's family. They had nine children. I loved them all, but I ran away from there pretty quickly. A teacher from my elementary school took me in as a foster child for a while. I ran away from there.

Between foster placements and juvenile detention, I'd be out on the street, where I felt safe. I did not want to be with adults. I did not trust any of them. I felt them judging me or feeling sorry for me. Or their kids got jealous when I took up their parents' time.

Why deal with any of that when I could blend into the wave of young people flocking to the city, with their long hair, braless breasts, bare feet, unshaven beards? I learned from them how to panhandle, steal, shoplift food, and disappear when the cops came close. I slept in the park, in the bushes. I slept in cars. I slept in telephone booths. Some of the street people took me under their wing, letting me sleep in corners of their crash pads. They were doing everything: marijuana, acid, mushrooms, speed, heroin— everything. I tried all of it. At thirteen, fourteen, fifteen, I did everything the streets of Dallas had to offer. Except sex. My street family kept an eye out for me. I don't know what they said or how they knew. Somehow the message got out: Don't mess with her. I did not have sex until I married Jenny's dad.

In juvenile detention, I kept running into Tink, the pretty little white girl I had staged a fight with on my first time through. "Hell yeah," she said. "I didn't blame you for that. Any way to get in solitary is a good way." We became friends.

She ran from her upper-middle-class family every chance she got. They tried to keep her off the streets. She loved drugs. She loved men. She wanted to try them all.

One day she said, "My dad's putting me in an upscale foster home. They have a maid, and you have your own room with one other person. Three squares a day, really good food. You get to go to school and they don't follow you there. They don't know what you're doing as long as you check in for dinner. It's nice." Hope Cottage was over in North Dallas, a hip part of town. Tink said, "I'm going to tell my dad to get you in there or I'm not going. He'll do it."

She did it! She got me into that fancy girls' home, in a two-story house with laid-back foster parents and a maid who cooked and also cleaned the common spaces. We had to keep our own rooms clean. We got an allowance. We got to smoke outside and swim in the pool out back. I thought I had it made.

Tink and I became inseparable for the six months we lived there. Though we set out for school in the morning, we seldom arrived at that destination. More often, we met up with old street connections, scored some drugs—LSD and crystal meth being our favorites—and tripped the days away. Tink found a boyfriend, Danny, only seventeen himself, who lived in an apartment with a roommate, David, who was a mellow guy, sweet and safe. David worked at Arby's to support himself and his skid row–drunk father; his mother had died several years earlier, the siblings scattered. He and I became friends, just friends, while Tink and her guy slipped off to the bedroom as often as not.

Of course we found trouble, or trouble found us. It did not take long.

We started tripping all the time, beyond what our allowance could bear. Tink figured she'd put us ahead of our own supply by getting a dealer to front her a hundred hits of LSD to sell at $10 a tab. We decided to sample the stash first, and while we were soaring high, we handed it out to all our friends, too. Within a few days, our supply had dwindled to almost nothing.

The dealer started laying for us when we would leave in the morning for school. He threatened Tink. "Get me my money. That, or I'll kill you."

David and Danny, hearing this and knowing that we could not put our hands on $1,000 anytime soon, convinced us to ditch Hope Cottage for their apartment and their protection. Tink and I both viewed that as a short-term solution. As seasoned runaways, we knew we could not call the shots on our foster placements.

When Tink and Danny headed straight out to Mexico to get married, as other kids we knew had done to free themselves from the system, David offered, "Why don't we do that? Then when you're out on the street, they can't pick you up." And so we took off for Mexico, with me as translator. When we returned to Dallas two days later, I was a married, legally emancipated fifteen-year-old.

David and I became lovers after marriage. He never pushed himself on me. We did a lot of acid together, and when you do that much acid, you can see things you do not usually see. I saw kindness in him. I saw a person I could trust.

Even so, before we consummated the marriage, we struck a flat-out deal. "I will do this only under one condition. You will never, ever tell me what I can and cannot do."

"Never," he said. "I love you."

We spent the next two years drugging and drinking and loving each other as well as two wounded young people could.

5

Dallas: Vision

A couple of years later, my life took another turn.

I had a vision. It came first in a dream. I saw myself standing at the top of a mountain, almost as if I were a tree rooted in the soil of that place. At the same time, I could see myself from above, from an eagle's eye, distant yet clear, arms outstretched toward the sky. A wild, uncharted scent pervaded the air, like the trace of every being, plant and animal, that had ever existed, pressed into one clear essence. I could hear below the city in apocalypse, with sirens screeching and bombs blasting, people moaning and animals—dogs, cats, horses—wailing as they stampeded through melting tar roads to escape the burning metropolis. I felt safe on the mountain.

Somehow, I knew this dream to be more than a dream, even the first time it came to me. In its urgent pull on every facet of my mind and senses, in its defiance of the boundaries of perspective and time, in its call to levels of my being beyond those I could name, I recalled my most intense experiences with psychedelics. I took psychedelics not to get high in an ordinary sense. I sought truth: transcendent, lucid, prophetic. Why are we here on this Earth? Why do we suffer? What are we supposed to be doing, and how are we supposed to do it? I had asked these questions since childhood, finding no answers whatsoever in the fire-and-brimstone sermons at the Baptist churches my mother sometimes dragged us to. LSD—and psilocybin, the magic mushrooms, even more sharply—allowed me to pierce the veil, to glimpse the world of the Spirit. I ached for that world and knew when I touched it. I did not flinch at its brilliance. I craved it more than anything in the material world. And so, I knew this dream to be a vision when it visited me, and I knew that it held the meanings, the map, of my life's path.

I also knew when I woke up that morning that I was pregnant. "We've got a baby coming," I told David. "We can't be doing drugs. Those mess a baby up."

We quit everything cold turkey. David, though, started drinking more, which sent him down a road he would never get off, however clearly he saw the wreckage ahead mirrored by his own father.

My brother Joe's wife, Sylvia, got pregnant around the same time. We lived near them, not far from my parents, all in the barrio. My mother would make the rounds to check on the pregnant ones. We never spoke out a reconciliation. We took up our roles as mother and married daughter with a grandchild on the way. Never mind that I was seventeen, my husband nineteen, neither of us in possession of a high school diploma or plans for our future.

"You will have a girl," she said. "Sylvia's will be a boy." She got that right, except that Sylvia had twins, born two weeks before my Jennifer Jo.

Quite soon into the pregnancy, maybe three months, Mom and Dad screeched up in their Buick one day before David got home from work. They had gotten a call from the hospital. Joe, again. They came for me automatically on these occasions. Something broken; something sliced; something stitched. Joe had been getting into trouble his whole life.

And I understood Joe better than anyone. He and I knew how it felt to make our way in the barrio, comprehending fully that the scraps thrown to us as school and jobs, the relentless poverty and violence and racism, were wrong. We raged. We fought back. We were the black sheep.

Dad sideswiped trashcans as he drove fiendishly through the purple dusk to Methodist Hospital, shouting, "What kind of man is my son, following the pachucos when he has a baby on the way? I will disown him, after I kill him!" Dad did not know that his eighteen-year-old son led our neighborhood gang, Los Altos. They were not pachucos. Pachucos carried guns and knives. Los Altos were just kids. They did not deal drugs. They kept our turf safe, drank beer when they could get their hands on it, smoked cigarettes, occasionally broke into a store, and got into fights with neighboring gangs trying to encroach on our turf.

We raced through the emergency department corridor. "Moroles!" Dad called out. "Where is he?"

A single bullet through the head from a .22 pistol. He looked alive; he felt warm. "Dead," is all the doctor said before leaving the room. No "sorry" or "we did all we could" or "let me get you a chair, ma'am" as Mom pitched herself onto her son's body and Dad folded to the floor, where he sat head in hands, rocking, until Mom sat by him and they sobbed for a long time. I stood beside my handsome brother in silence.

Something shifted in me as I looked from my stilled brother to my broken parents. I returned to them. I forgave them. I had no choice but to forgive them. They were as confused as I was. We were all children. None of us knew the way through this pain. I simply let them back into my heart.

Joe's murder blew a hole through all of us. It made no sense. It never would. Another kid, imagining Joe had been messing around with his girlfriend, had fired a single shot. Joe never saw it coming.

It messed me up. Seventeen and pregnant, I began to duck unseen bullets as cars drove by me. Other members of Los Altos—who had loved and followed my funny, strong, beautiful brother—became my bodyguards. Why had he not dodged that one bullet?

Mom and Dad left Dallas after the funeral, back to Rockport, Texas, with Diane, Lalo, and Suzanna. Just before Sylvia brought the fatherless twins into the world, they returned, patched back together, needing to love the new Moroles babies.

We stayed in Dallas two years after Jenny's birth, David and I. We worked at minimum-wage jobs. Some, like the landscaping gig at the Texas State Fair, afforded me the pleasure of working outside, in nature, where I felt free. Mom helped watch Jenny and the twins, Joe Jr. and John Michael. I went to night school for my GED.

After the birth, I went back to smoking some pot. Occasionally I dropped acid, alone or with David. Everything had changed. The soul-punch of my brother's murder, the surge of pure love for my baby girl, the cord of compassion for my parents, and the relentless return of that dream, the vision of a mountain wilderness where I could be free of the city's horrors and destruction, where I could see clear for miles, and peer into hazier dimensions—all of this combined in me as a call, an urgent call to search out my purpose and path through life.

I told only one person about the dream: my mother. She closed her eyes as I described the vividness, the quality of light and sound, the perception of another realm. I could not liken the experience to an acid trip in the telling, of course. Instead, I told her, "If Jesús had this dream, he could sculpt it. Amá Angelita could have sung it. Words can't describe it."

"These dreams will come to you, as they come to me," she said. "Amá Angelita sings to you. The Ancestors speak to you. You must learn how to listen, *mija*. We bear this burden."

✦ ✦ ✦

My first attempt to find guidance on this path brought me to a man named José Silva, a former radio and television repairman who had developed a course in psychic healing. He later gained fame and fortune with the patented Silva Mind Control technique based on his understanding of electricity and other forms of energy. I found Silva in Dallas in the early '70s, when he taught the course personally, handing out "Certified Psychic Healer" cards to those of us who completed the training. I later realized that his teachings, like those of many other mystics, Eastern and Western, sought only to quiet the chattering mind to allow other forms of energy to surface.

On the radio one night, while under the influence of acid, I heard a guru from India, Swami Satchidananda, speak about yoga as a way of life, a pathway toward inner peace and healing. Something about his spoken voice touched me. When he chanted the vast, open sound of "om"—which he described as the divine sound of the universe—I began spontaneously to chant with him. The vibrations of the om sound both calmed and energized me, in much the same way as my vision of the mountain.

I went out the next day in search of a yoga studio. Famous as he was after appearing at Woodstock in 1969, Satchidananda did not yet have a center in Dallas. Finally, I did come across a place at the corner of Lemon and Oaklawn, a tiny studio with a spiritual bookstore and an Indian grocery attached. A married couple, Ranjana and Kumar Pallana, ran the place, offering yoga and meditation instruction as well as massage.

Ranjana became my teacher. Seeing that I had no money to pay for classes, sensing my fire to learn everything she could possibly teach me, she let me exchange work for my yoga classes.

Ranjana practiced as a master massage healer, combining bodywork techniques with yogic healing practices. Dallas straggled behind the coasts, or even the big college towns like Austin, which had a sizeable alternative scene. Even so, my time on the streets of Dallas had stripped me of the extreme modesty of my parents' home. Going braless, skinny-dipping, nursing babies in public—none of this shocked me anymore. Still, I felt relieved that Ranjana worked only with female massage clients, referring males to Kumar for treatment.

Between massage clients, Ranjana let me clean the room, change the sheets, add a new cone of incense to the ceramic pot. After instructing each client to disrobe and lie on the massage table covered with a light sheet, I would leave the room for a moment or two. On return, I oiled the person up, just a little bit, honoring an unspoken code of modesty that left the body covered as my hands discreetly spread the lightly scented ayurvedic oil.

Ranjana's clientele seemed heavy on dancers, people I might now recognize as exotic dancers, or outside the mainstream in one way or another. Some arrived for their sessions in clothing that seemed fit for the stage, exaggerated in frills and feathers, sometimes leather. A fair number of this lot did not give a hoot about the hushed decorum I tried to establish. They were the good tippers, too.

I will never forget Misty, the dancer who stood butt naked when I walked back into the room, her breasts jutting out about a foot from her delicate frame. I stood there, feeling a warm blush creep up my neck, unable to say my few words of instruction.

"Oh, honey, they're not real," she said. "Come on over here. Have a feel." She laughed loud and hard as I—stick-thin, small-breasted—stepped over to touch.

When I wasn't busy, I would stop to watch Ranjana in practice. I understood that her massage work involved more than the physical, more than the eye could behold. She had a keen interest in the mystic and esoteric. In later years, people would call her approach to healing "holistic." I observed closely.

One afternoon she said, "Can you rub my shoulders? My arms are tired. Rub my shoulders a little bit, María Cristina." I started rubbing her shoulders, focusing my mind and intuition, or what I was coming to call my psychic abilities, on her.

After a few minutes, she stopped me. She put her hand on mine and turned to me with great feeling, "We have got to teach you. You have a gift, a special gift."

From then on, I apprenticed myself to Ranjana in earnest. Over the next two years, she taught me everything she could. Massage practice required no license back then.

One day I told her of a dream in which a brown-skinned man, sitting in a lotus position and wearing only the white cloth of an Indian mystic, appeared to me. Ranjana pulled a dog-eared book from her shelves. "Is it this man?" I nodded. "Bhagavan Nityananda appeared to you. He is no longer living. His disciple carries forth his lineage and his powers. Yes, Swami Muktananda has come to America, and he will speak in Dallas next week."

Ranjana brought me to hear Muktananda speak about his Siddha Yoga path. After that, I started going with her to different speeches and workshops, as a wave of wisdom from the East drifted into Dallas in the early '70s. Ranjana also opened to me her personal library of works on meditation, yoga, mysticism, and psychic healing. I immersed myself, reading more than I could process through my mind. I moved toward the messages and messengers who reached me at the deepest levels. I felt that I had stepped onto a path, a spiritual path I wanted passionately to follow, for my own survival at the very least.

From Paramahansa Yogananda's *Autobiography of a Yogi*, I learned the Majestic Promise of the Bhagavad Gita, ancient Hindu scripture, which I understood to translate as "even a tiny bit of this real religion protects one from great fear (the colossal sufferings inherent in the repeated cycles of birth and death)." To this day, I carry the knowledge that I can keep my head when danger faces me. By focusing inwardly on the meaning of the words of the Majestic Promise and repeating to myself out loud or silently the sounds of the ancient Sanskrit words themselves—*Swalpamapyasya dharmasya trayate mahato bhayat*—I can calm and center myself. I can breathe my way out of panic even in situations of immediate threat.

♪ ♪ ♪

One cold, rainy night as I stood at the bus stop after my GED class, a young man I had seen in class pulled over. "I can give you a lift," he said. "Awful night." I hopped in.

When I saw that he was going to take me down a dark road, not the right way, I knew I had made a bad choice. I began to chant silently.

He let me know he planned to have sex with me, one way or another.

I spoke from the calm core of my being. "You don't want to do this. You will have to kill me first, because I'm not going to do this again. I've been down this road before and I'm not doing it. I don't understand why you're doing it. Look at you. You're handsome. Young. Why would you want to force yourself on someone that doesn't want to?" I said all this calmly. "I'm married. I have a little girl waiting for me at home."

I could see him hesitate. But then he pulled out a knife and put it to my throat. "I *will* kill you."

I chanted silently as I talked him down. "Why would you want to do that? You need to take care of yourself. This isn't what you want on your life, to hurt somebody like that."

He drove me home, alive and unharmed. I went in to hug my Jenny and hold her hand. Then I went to bed, pressed up next to David. I chanted my gratitude to the Universe.

At one point, I managed to secure a spot for Jenny in a pre–Head Start program that provided free daycare to women trying to get back to work. The woman who ran the place helped me to land a job in a bilingual Head Start program for older children. That is where I met Leona Garcia, the tiny, raven-haired, dark-skinned, Mayan-looking woman around my age who would become one of the housemates David and I invited in to make the rent and share the space of a small collective household in East Dallas.

Leona would accompany me on several adventures over the years. My spiritual yearning led me into unknown spaces and places; Leona sought companionship. She had left El Paso at a young age, feeling herself a late-comer and interloper in her large family. Jenny and I became her *familia*; David less so, as he staggered into the abyss of alcoholism.

It didn't take much convincing to get Leona to hitchhike with me to seek a personal audience with Swami Muktananda at his ashram in Oakland,

California. I had been smoking pot pretty steadily since I was fourteen years old. I had, in fact, been dealing in quantities large enough to supply our habit and supplement David's dwindling, uncertain income. I wanted to stop. I felt sure that Muktananda could help me.

Leona watched me roll up a big old joint, which I positioned carefully in a satin-lined jewelry box that looked like a miniature casket. I snapped the little coffin shut and we hit the road.

We found the ashram swarming with upper-class, uptight white kids who informed me that I'd need to fork up a few hundred dollars for the upcoming meditation retreat if I wanted to get anywhere close to Muktananda.

"They don't even know how to wipe their own asses," I told Leona. "We'll figure this out."

First of all, the ashram held free meditation sessions. At the end of each session, people filed past the swami, who perched on a plush pillow in the front of the room, peacock feather in hand.

I paused before him, holding out my jewelry-box casket. Slowly, I opened the hinged cover to reveal the overstuffed joint. Muktananda got it immediately. He threw his head back in laughter, and before his stunned acolytes could stop him, he rose from his pillow to wrap me in a firm embrace, while his holy brats tried to push me along through the line.

Each day I attended the free meditations. I observed the layout of the ashram, took note of the daily schedule. Each day I asked for a scholarship, a discount, a way to work off the cost of the retreat. Each day they said, "No way. Get the money or get out of here."

Finally I told Leona, "I'm going to try something."

I had been watching how they did things at the ashram. The swami took walks in the morning before breakfast, then slipped into a room right off the auditorium. That's my chance, I told myself. If I could get him alone in that room, I knew I could convince him to allow me into the retreat, to receive the special initiation he dispensed only there.

I edged into the solid darkness of the room, shutting the door behind me. My eyes adjusted to reveal his silhouette lying on the bed. Total stillness.

Suddenly he switched on the light by his bed, grabbed his cane, and lunged at me. I saw the flicker of recognition in his eyes as I ducked the cane and lit out of the room, down the aisle, out of the building.

"Getting closer," I told Leona, who was shyly along for the ride, as long as she could stay back at our crash pad smoking the deceased joint and others. "Tonight, we'll go to the evening meditation in disguise."

I wrapped a sari over my head, around my body, as I had seen women at the ashram do. With my head bowed, I shuffled meekly with the crowd to approach the guru on his pillow for a tap of the peacock feather.

The second he saw me, he knew me. He stood up, laughing, extending his arms, pulling me into a hug. Unlike the first time he touched me without the feather as a shock absorber, I felt the full power of the universal energy—the Shakti, which the swami channeled—as it coursed through every cell of my body with an indescribable, deeply uncomfortable surge. My knees buckled.

The ashramites descended, pushing me roughly through the line. A pudgy bearded one, pasty-skinned and pissed off, broke the ashram's hush to say, "We told you before: no money, no Shakti. Don't come back here."

Muktananda sat back on his pillow. He spoke quietly to his bouncers: "She will need care for three days. She will be our guest at the ashram for this cleansing. You will tend to her lovingly. Then she will be my own special guest at the retreat this weekend."

So it was. For three days, a fever gripped me as my body purged all manner of impurities and the silenced devotees did as they had been told. At the weekend retreat, the swami affirmed that in making a pilgrimage all the way from Texas, I had demonstrated a great thirst for spiritual growth, an urgency. Life is precious, he taught, and the quest for spiritual wisdom must be urgent. Do what you need to do in this life now. Do what you came here to do, and then leave in a good way.

Since that weekend, I have had no active desire to smoke pot. When I sit around people who are getting high, I might get a contact high. If they try to pass to me, I usually just pass to the next person. Muktananda's initiation allowed me to make that leap.

♪ ♪ ♪

Soon after that, Swami Muktananda gave me an infinitely greater gift. He led me back home, to my people.

"Muktananda will be in Oklahoma soon," Ranjana informed me. "We must go. He will be with the medicine men and women of your people."

Strangely, I did not stop to think what Ranjana meant by "my people." My hunger for Muktananda's spiritual wisdom felt insatiable. I would go anywhere to be in his presence again.

A girl named Mike, also a yoga student, drove with Ranjana and me to a retreat at a Salvation Army campground near Oklahoma City. Scores of people attended, including many Indian medicine people and elders from the Five Civilized Tribes. I met there Phillip Deere, the Muscogee Creek medicine man and American Indian Movement activist who would later become an important mentor for me. I experienced Ceremony for the first time. And I was stunned into silence, the deep true silence of recognition, when I witnessed the tan-skinned Indians, dressed in traditional robes and regalia, forge a Ceremonial bond of brotherhood with the tan-skinned Swami Muktananda, dressed in the robes of his tradition, as they inducted him through a ritual adoption into the tribe. My people.

"You are proud first because you are an Indian," said my father.

"The Ancestors speak to you. You must learn how to listen," said my mother. "We bear this burden."

"You have a gift, a special gift," said Ranjana.

As I looked around the circle, from one bronzed face to the next, one robed healer sharing breath and wisdom with the next, in the protection of the Ancestors, under the warmth of our Father Sun, on the body of our Mother Earth, I could only weep. My people. Home.

Sometimes I would take off for the weekend, leaving Jenny with my parents. That is how I coped. I would have to get away, to get out, to blow things out of my head. I would hitchhike to Austin, where I had friends. We would hang out on the strip, Guadalupe Street.

One of those weekends, rain fell steadily. I was staying outside with the other street people. A young hippie couple came through with sandwiches for all of us. When they saw that I was not doing so well, shivering out in the rain, they invited me to their house for a dry night's sleep.

"We're moving to Arkansas next week," they told me. "Up in the Ozark Mountains."

"Arkansas?"

"It's open land there. Come and stay. Everything is free. Everyone is welcome. Just come there and live. Everyone shares. Men and women and babies. Clean air, peace, and love."

"Arkansas?"

"So remote the cops couldn't find you if they wanted to. Or the straight people. Bring your weed. Park at the bottom of the mountain and follow the old logging road up about two miles. You can stand on top of that mountain and see forever."

They were describing my dream, the vision that came to me almost nightly. Arkansas?

"The community is called Sassafras. First go to Fayetteville, where the university is," they said. "People from the commune go to the co-op there every week or so to get food. Go there and we'll show up."

I returned to Dallas intoxicated with the news. How many times had I told David about my dream? Or my mother? How often had Ranjana heard me describe that mountaintop vision? Where *was* that mountain? I had waited and waited for its meaning to become clear.

Now I knew. Arkansas!

6

O Arkansas!

We rumbled into Fayetteville, Arkansas, in late spring of 1973 in a '65 Chevy van top-loaded with our possessions, padded with carpeting for comfortable sleep, and repainted a dark green that earned it the nickname "Pickle." Jenny, almost three years old by then, gasped at the picture-book beauty of the college town, with its maples and dogwoods in bloom. "Fairy town," she named it.

We slept in the van for a few days as we got the lay of the land, soon realizing that the money I had saved could just barely afford us a small place on the south side of Fayetteville, in the historically Black neighborhood of the overwhelmingly white, racially segregated town. David landed a freelance carpentry job within a week, and the older woman next door welcomed Jenny into her informal daycare. When other neighbors invited us to their backyard barbeque, where beer flowed and weed wafted, we knew we would be okay in Fayetteville, Arkansas.

I, meanwhile, made my way to the food co-op, as my Austin acquaintances had suggested. An old converted train station on West Street, with tracks running behind, housed both the co-op and the Summercorn Natural Bakery & Café. The folks at the co-op sent me over to the bakery, which just so happened to be hiring.

I plunged headlong into a new way of life. I had been drifting that way in Dallas with Ranjana, as on the streets, even if I had not put a name to it all yet. On my visits to Austin and to California, I had certainly seen young people shedding conventions and constraints and clothing. I would soon shed with the best of them.

Everything seemed to come into question in the alternative community: Who to live with, and how. How to make collective decisions. What to do for work and money. Whether money mattered. What to wear, if anything. What to eat. What gods to worship, and how, and if; or was the body the Holy Land? Which laws to observe, which to resist. How to treat the Earth. How to heal. How to love. How to raise children. How to be like children again, spontaneous and full of wonder.

In Fayetteville, back-to-the-landers flooded into town for provisions and services, sometimes for work. They tended to be young, middle-class white people originally from suburbs or cities, as often from distant as from local places. They bought cheap acreage in the Ozarks, thinking they would farm or get by as crafters of pottery or earrings or granola or whatever else they could sell. Some formed communes. Some made a go of it on the land and remain there to this day. Others drifted back to towns and cities, college and more schooling, 9-to-5 routines and regular paychecks, or small businesses catering to the hip community. At the time, I perceived only that these long-haired, nature-loving people were living my dream, my vision of liberation on a mountaintop far from the chaos of the city.

When the couple I had met back in Austin rambled into Summercorn one day, my heart leapt.

Within days, David, Jenny, and I set out in the Pickle with detailed directions to the Sassafras community, some sixty-five miles away in Newton County. As we headed out Highway 16, the rolling hills gradually built into mountains. The minute we turned on to Cave Mountain Road, leading into Boxley, I knew we had found the mountain of my dreams. We then climbed eleven miles up a fairly wide dirt road. Dust churned under our tires, leaving a haze behind us. Ahead we saw only green: lush ferns and towering hardwood trees layered with summer leaves. Sometimes the glint of a runoff mountain stream sparked through the foliage, giving the trek up the rugged logging road an otherworldly radiance.

Off the road every half mile or so we saw small wooden structures, many of them more like hunting cabins than homes. Only the patched-up cars around them, plus a few scraggly goats and dogs, suggested that people currently lived in these shacks. After about eight or ten miles, we came to a gathering of well-established farmhouses. The respected Fowler family inhabited this hamlet, we later learned, along with "hill people" scratching it out as hunters and loggers, crafters and canners, artists and musicians, most wanting nothing to do with the outsiders further up the hill.

We missed the turnoff to Sassafras, then doubled back to an even more rutted road, rocky and rough, barely passable. At the one-mile mark, we arrived at an open gate with a sloppily handwritten sign reading, "No Trepasing." I caught the misspelling.

"We're here! We're here!" Jenny could hardly contain her excitement as we approached the commune's parking area. To her, the clutter of junked cars, empty beer cans, rusted rolls of fencing, countless cigarette butts, and other random heaps of trash meant nothing.

We parked the Pickle and headed toward the main structure, a two-story wooden homestead jacked up on piers, with weathered oak siding and three tall stairs, no railing, leading inside. Several long-haired men and women sat in the front room passing a joint. No one said a word to us as we drifted through to the kitchen, where some women were preparing what looked like a huge pot of soup. Finally, one of them looked our way, unsmiling: "Who are you? What are you doing here?"

I explained that our friends had invited us out for a visit.

"They're not here," she said, casting a look at Jenny, who, unfazed by the grunginess of the people and place, darted curiously from room to room.

After standing about uncomfortably for a couple of minutes, we made our way back outside. We observed a few sweaty people working in a vegetable garden. At least a dozen others milled about. Another clutch sat around a cold fire pit, drinking beer and smoking.

"We don't belong here," I said to David. "They've trashed my mountain. They're just farting around here. Let's go."

It took me over a year to return to Sassafras, this time with Leona, who had by then moved to Fayetteville.

✦✦✦

A year can be more than a collection of moon cycles. As Diana Rivers—the heiress who bought the land that held Sassafras and then Arco Iris—would later write in one of her lesbian fantasy novels, it was as if a magical comet had passed over the region, instantly awakening a host of women to a new awareness, new sexuality, new desire to love other women. Just like that.

In Fayetteville that first winter, David and I could not scrape the money together to turn on the gas. I poured cayenne pepper into my socks to generate heat, as I remembered my father doing when he went hunting. It took an hour of soaking my blazing feet in a tub of cold water to put out the flame.

David's income became more haphazard as his alcohol intake escalated. He did day-labor and carpentry jobs. Often, he returned home drunk. Sometimes he got soused before leaving the house for a job. Many times, he left to grab cigarettes or a beer and did not show up until the next day. One time, he took Jenny with him and didn't return until the next morning. That, on top of nearly killing us all in the car the week before, did it for me. Frightened, furious, heartbroken, I told David that I loved him but that he had to go. My baby was everything. I protected her in every way. He was big enough to take care of himself; she was not. I sent David packing, back to Dallas in our one vehicle to stay with my sister and our community. He had a place to go. It had to be.

I just kept working, with the dream of saving up to buy some land on that mountain. Maybe, I thought, maybe that's what is meant to happen. Leona moved in with Jenny and me, while another transplanted Dallas friend, Judy Robinson, gave Jenny a scholarship to her Montessori school. We needed little, and we got by.

The food co-op and Summercorn Natural Bakery & Café thrived as Fayetteville's alternative scene grew. The two businesses launched an all-women's interstate trucking business for natural foods, and all moved together to a big warehouse building behind Dickson Street, the main drag near the university. Each of the businesses ran as a collective, including a little alternative bookstore stocked mostly with women's books and a thrift store that also featured locally made crafts.

From what I could tell, everyone in the collective was white except me, with one possible exception: Patti Cardozo, who later took the name Shiner. I could not quite place her ethnically, with her slightly olive-toned skin and long, wildly curly dark hair. Later I learned of her Sephardic Jewish heritage. To me, she of all the middle-class people in the collective (and Shiner was that, if not upper-class) seemed different—less arrogant, and kind.

Shiner and I had been working together at the bakery for some time, earning our $1.25 an hour and enjoying our quiet 4 a.m. shift, when I sent David off. She had already been offering me rides to and from work, seeing that we had only one vehicle in our family. With David's departure, she made that a regular practice. She would pick me up in her old funky Valiant, with her little rat terrier, Woofies, riding shotgun. We laughed easily together. We laughed and joked while kneading dough or mixing granola or rolling out pastry. After work, she would hang out at my place as I cleaned house and prepared dinner. Then she would drive me to get Jenny from daycare.

Both Jenny and I took it hard when Shiner left one day to see her folks in San Francisco for a visit of unspecified length. A month went by with no word. Then she sent pictures of her hippie wedding to an old boyfriend. A few weeks later, she wrote about their divorce. Not too long after that, she showed up in Fayetteville declaring herself a lesbian, soon to be joining the now all-lesbian trucking collective.

I could have gotten whiplash trying to wrap my head around these rapid-fire developments. But that is how it seemed in Fayetteville at that time. One day, all these women were in the alternative community with their male partners; some had young kids. The next day they had come out, chopped their hair off, and become the most separatist of separatists. Even Shiner chopped off her long, dark, beautiful curls in those early days of her lesbian journey.

In a matter of weeks, she convinced me to quit the bakery and join the women's trucking collective. Except that the other women in the collective did not want me there. "You're not a lesbian," they said. That was true.

"You all weren't lesbians a month ago, either," Shiner argued. That was true, too.

They relented, and I began my training as a long-haul semitruck driver, working one week on, one week off on a two-person team with Shiner, delivering natural foods to co-ops and health food stores on a central United States run. We went as far north as Michigan and Wisconsin, and everywhere in between, lifting fifty-pound bags and boxes, and sometimes fending off men who seemed to consider my long, flowing hair an invitation to harass us. With our shirtsleeves rolled up over bulging muscles, we warded them off pretty quickly.

Jenny stayed at Moon House, a safe house for children, during these runs. Feather ran Moon House on the south side of Fayetteville, taking care of lesbian workers' children overnight. She did not quiz me about my sexuality, unlike many of the white, middle-class, newly minted lesbians in town, who claimed to be "political" and hip, eager for "diversity," but were nonetheless ready to jab and judge when faced with an actual working-class woman of color who did not have family funds appear magically when the bills came due, or a college education, or any other perks of privileged white existence rolling in. Feather let us be.

In Shiner, I found a friend of the heart. Our backgrounds could not have been more different. She spoke of a summer home on a lake and private schools. Her parents had moved from Minneapolis to San Francisco, where they owned two artsy bookstores in the Castro District. She was soft-spoken and funny. Her comments about sex often made me blush. She felt comfortable in her body. She took risks and feared little. Shiner lived full tilt. I should have known that she would die young.

I fell hard and fully and naturally in love with that woman. When our nights in the cabin of the truck progressed from cuddling to lovemaking, at her initiation, I hardly registered a shift. I had no clear moment of realization, no lesbian epiphany or declaration. My heart led the way.

Soon, in my time with Indigenous communities across the Americas, I would learn the term "Two Spirit." I am one of those they call a Two Spirit. I am right in the middle. I can love anybody, male or female. I fall in love with the being. Our way of belief is that all of us are masculine and feminine by nature. Some women are more masculine. Some women are more feminine. And then there are some like me, in the middle. I can go either way. I am a Libra, balanced between two sides. I am a Two-Spirit woman. I lead with my heart.

Shiner, on the other hand, went all in with the emerging lesbian separatist community not only in Fayetteville but also out on Cave Mountain. Out there, the women had tossed the men off the land, come out as lesbians, and proclaimed Sassafras as women's land. Diana Rivers, who had bought the land originally with an inheritance from a wealthy cousin, held true to her communal values: She placed ownership of the land in the collective hands of the seven women currently committed to being there. Shiner happened to be among them.

My dream of the mountain persisted. Even after the deeply disappointing day trip there with David and Jenny, the vision stayed clear. If anything, I sensed more strongly than ever the land, the air, the rocks, the plants, the wildlife, the vista of that mountain—not a generic mountain, but that very place, *my mountain*—calling me. Only the human inhabitants repelled me; as in the dream, they took on a menacing presence, almost witchlike in black capes. This vision, which had come to me in my sleep since Dallas, became a waking vision, too, like a painting with color and detail filling in gradually. I yearned to touch its surfaces. I knew I could not. Not yet.

Shiner kept at me. "It's women's land now. It's nothing like what you saw. Women are closer to the Earth. Women understand nature. Everything there has changed. You'll see. I urge you to give it another chance."

Also a Libra, Shiner had Taurus rising, meaning she had a bit of the bull in her. Direct and insistent, she could be contagiously optimistic, as white people can afford to be.

I had my doubts. A number of women in the trucking collective and other lesbian collectives in town spent time out at Sassafras. All of them white, most of them middle-class, they had swung hard toward separatism, rejecting anything connected to "the patriarchy": men, male children, male gods, straight women, bisexual women, "feminine" styles of hair and clothing. Some went so far as to reject all children, and the role of motherhood itself, as an exploitation of women's bodies and labor. Those who did not scorn me outright for my refusal to send Jenny off so that I could immerse myself in the separatist revolution still treated me with a standoffish air of superiority. Although I was around the same age as most of these women— early to mid-twenties—I had some living under my belt already. I had little patience for them.

Because I loved Shiner and trusted her, I finally made another trip to Sassafras. Leona accompanied me.

Right at the gate, two towering, muscular women stopped us. "Who are you? What do you all want?"

"I'm Shiner's partner," I said. "We're just here for a visit."

"She's not here." They sneered but let us pass. The parking area still looked like a junkyard. I noticed several new, partially built makeshift shacks on the way to the structure marked "Main House," along with a few lean-to tents. Many women roamed about, none greeting us. Some went topless. Some wore only a breechcloth and a belt. Several, I noted, had knives tucked into their belts. A few wore beaded, feathered headbands and moccasins.

They watched us as we made our way to the Main House. We passed the fire pit I had seen the year before, still surrounded by beer drinkers and tobacco or weed smokers, who seemed as sweaty and unfriendly as the last batch. The garden looked better tended, and the Main House, once we got inside, seemed a little cleaner. But other than the switching out of the long-haired men for a bunch of short-haired women, I could not see all that much change.

As Leona and I—two Indian women, one short, one tall; one dark-skinned, one light; both with long, straight black hair, and both saddened by the spectacle—trudged back toward our truck, a sturdy woman with close-cropped white-blond hair approached us. "My name is Berry," she said. She had a strong German accent. "I saw you here the last time you came. You belong here. You do belong here. Don't go away."

"We don't belong here. We're not wanted here. This is not our way."

"You do belong here," she insisted. She fastened her clear-blue eyes on me.

"No, we could never live here amongst y'all."

"There's more land on the other side of the creek. I can tell you how to get there." She gave us a brief outline of a course through the wilderness to the smaller mountain on the other side of Route 21. That land, too, had been purchased by Diana Rivers. Not one person lived there. "You could be safe there."

Berry gave me a renewed sense of hope that somewhere in these mountains we could live in peace. My heart opened a crack.

We left it at that.

⁄ ⁄ ⁄

Hepatitis, the infectious type you can get from food, hit Fayetteville a few weeks later. It ravaged the alternative community, starting with the café, skipping over to the bakery, and working its way through the food co-op, the bookstore, the warehouse, and the trucking collective. One by one, people fell critically ill. I was the last driver standing.

Shiner and other hepatitis-stricken lesbians went out to Sassafras to heal. The women there set up the Main House as a makeshift infirmary, where the healthy cared for the sick until the roles needed to be reversed. Just about everyone caught it.

I told Shiner, "If I get it, do not take me out to Sassafras. And do not take me to a hospital. The only place I want to be is home. I don't care what happens; leave me at home."

Somehow, I seemed to avoid infection, maybe because I was doing consecutive trucking runs instead of spending my off week at the warehouse around the contagion. I went for weeks without a break. My extreme exhaustion seemed reasonable given the workload.

Then one day, Shiner, semi-recovered, received a phone call from Jenny, almost five years old by then. "My mom is passed out on the floor."

I do not recall when Shiner swooped in with Briar, a six-foot-two, massively strong trucker, who scooped me up in her arms and carried me to her van. Out cold with fever at that point, I woke up as Briar deposited me in the Main House at Sassafras.

Several women lay on mattresses there, moaning and writhing in pain. "This is exactly what I told you not to do," I hissed at Shiner.

"I knew I'd need help taking care of you." She looked terrified.

Berry, the immigrant from Germany, who was a registered nurse, said, "I'm living in the Pottery Shed. I'll fix up a space in there, and we'll take you out there. Will you stay if we take you out there and I take care of you? I'll take care of you."

I could barely speak. I do not know if I agreed or not. Everything went black again.

In the Pottery Shed, I became sicker and sicker over the next days. Fever and pain possessed me. Hepatitis had struck me before, when I lived on the streets in Dallas; my weakened liver now struggled to function. My skin and eyes turned yellow. I could scarcely lift a limb as Berry and Shiner tended to my most basic needs: drinking, toileting, shifting of position to avoid bedsores.

Shiner broke. She had not been hardened by life. She cried and cried as I grew weaker. "I've got to leave here," she said. "I can't watch."

I told her to take Jenny from Moon House to my parents' home in Dallas. She did that. From there, she took off to the West Coast with Briar, leaving me with a new, heavily embroidered white-cotton caftan to wear as a burial gown.

Over the next days, Berry begged me to go to the hospital. I refused. I recalled Parkland Hospital, where they had overdosed me with Thorazine, causing me to relive the rape that had derailed life as I knew it. "I'd rather die," I told her. "Let me die."

I tried to escape when Berry left the Pottery Shed one day. I wound barefoot over flat, frozen ground, imagining how to get to Highway 21. Fever and a desperation to leave Sassafras propelled me. I stumbled a few dozen yards down the icy path. A voice, a woman's voice, spoke inside and outside my head. *Go back, go back.* I turned back. At one point I crawled in the snow. I had left the shed door open. The floor had chilled. Berry had returned. Her arms felt like a soft blanket as she lifted me back onto the mattress.

I drifted in and out, in and out. I heard Berry's voice: "She is dying." I heard sounds outside, women keening and drumming. I heard Berry sob, low.

I drew a deep breath, a different breath, and felt my body release the air, slowly and with finality. A beautiful older Indian woman with long white braids appeared, dressed in white Ceremonial robes. *My name is Santa María*, she said. *You are not going to die. You are resting and you will be going back. You will start anew. Your new life will begin. You have a path that you will walk. Now just rest.*

7

SunHawk

In the stillness between the eternal here and there, I took in a breath. Sound and light bathed each cell of my body, silent, unseen, outside of time. I felt nothing: no pain, no fear. I opened my eyes to light—radiant, brilliant, brighter than it could possibly be.

Berry stood over me, her mouth wide with surprise. Tears wet her face. She later told me that a light had illuminated my body, and that she too felt her fear wash away.

"It's a new day," I said. "I have to go outside!"

"No, María Cristina. You're too weak."

"I have to go outside. I have to see this day. This new day. I have to see this new day." I tried to rise from the mattress as Berry wrapped the white burial caftan around me and tried to stuff my feet into some of her old slippers. "I don't want shoes!"

"There's snow on the ground," she protested. And then more severely, "You will let me get the others and tell them you're alive."

They made a pallet for me out on the snow. I felt no pain, no cold, as I floated barefoot over whitest snow, under bluest sky, all newborn and dazzling.

As I sat on the pallet, I looked off toward the north, toward our sister mountain, where I now live. There, on a high painted bluff, I saw three Indian warriors, wearing fringed leather leggings and mounted bareback on three beautiful, tall horses. The figure in the center waved a feathered medicine staff in a high circle, beckoning me to come.

Santa María, the old Indian woman who had led me through the tunnel of death and rebirth, appeared before me again in her white robes. *You have come far,* she said. *I have been with you. Now I leave. You will remember my words. Look toward the north. You must reclaim that land. There you will heal yourself and all who come to you. There you will build a sanctuary for all women, all children of the rainbow, all who come in peace to seek refuge. You will relearn from our Mother Earth the ways of the Ancestors. You are reborn to this Rainbow Land, Arco Iris. This is your path. Walk in strength. Walk in beauty, my sister.*

As Santa María faded into the light, I became aware gradually of my surroundings. The hard pallet. The delicious, pure cold air. My body, warm in the caftan. My feet on the frozen planks. Backed up against the Pottery Shed, the white women hovered, fear on their faces.

Hearing the rustle of many wings, I looked up to see a dozen buzzards circling darkly above me. Suddenly, from the south a single hawk shot through the air, piercing the death birds' circle, screeching a battle cry as it flew across our Father Sun, its red tail illuminated like a flame.

I now knew my medicine name: SunHawk. I knew my path.

Several years later, my mother told me she had seen it all happen. She saw me die on a mountain, surrounded by a dozen witches. "I was so afraid for you," she said. "I said many prayers for you."

The Sassafras women did not want me there. My physical condition frightened them. Painfully thin and of yellowish hue, I am sure I looked closer to death than I felt in my new state of wonder. A few days later, Berry got me dressed. Diana Rivers stuffed a plane ticket and a wad of ten hundred-dollar bills into my shirt pocket. They had decided to send me to an Indian medicine woman in New Mexico. Zulema. I had heard of her, a Two-Spirit woman from Nicaragua.

On the way out to New Mexico, I flew through Dallas, where I kept missing my connection. At last, I called my sister Diane and David for help. "You've got to get me on this plane." They came to the airport and saw me. "You look like David Bowie or the living dead," Diane said. I took out the roll of bills and gave one to each of them. They assured me that Jenny was fine, and they got me on the plane.

I stayed with Zulema only briefly. We clashed. I seemed to be in the way of her entourage of fawning white women. Within days, she took me out to Medicine Wheel, her land base in New Mexico, where she had a neighbor, an old Black Indian woman with gray hair in braids, by the name of Vicky Cryer. Vicky and her disabled mother lived in the desert in two adjoining trailers, where they took care of seven foster children, all Black. Though she took me in because Zulema told her to, she could see plainly that I needed help. I stayed there for about a month, eating and sleeping, eating and sleeping, regaining my strength. Vicky encouraged me to do a little more each day. I thanked her from my heart and with several of Diana's crisp bills.

Then I caught one of the health-food collective's trucks back to Fayetteville. The desert in bloom had to be the most beautiful sight I had ever seen, a rainbow of wildflower groundcover on rolling hills, with the occasional grand cactus standing guard. I took great pleasure in the view, though I yearned for my mountain, my sanctuary, my refuge.

Berry brought me there. I left my 350 Honda motorcycle in the shed at Sassafras. With no real road coming up to this land, not even a path, we made our way gingerly from Cave Mountain, climbing down one steep gorge and up another, over huge boulders covered in thick green moss; past towering beech, oak, hickory, and walnut trees and hundreds of wild magnolias; through Beech Creek's icy, jade-colored water to a steep upward climb of the gorge on the other side; until finally, as darkness descended, we saw at the top a small clearing, about the size of my garden now.

This was the land that had called me. Arco Iris. Rainbow Land. I knew upon seeing it. This land had called me through my sleep. It had called me through my dreams. It had called me through visions, as I lay dying and as I came back to life. I felt that the Spirits of the Land wanted me here.

I knelt on the sun-soaked earth to ask the Spirits of the Land and my Ancestors to help me recover this sacred ground. "Help me. Guide me, por favor. Ayúdame."

I still had a HUD-subsidized house in Fayetteville with most of a year's lease remaining on it. That became my base, where I gathered materials to bring to the land. I began to shed most of our possessions; they would have no purpose on my new path. The trucking company paid me a disability check; out of that, I bought a pup tent and a few other supplies, fueled up my little motorcycle. Then I headed out to Newton County, my "new town."

The old logging road that led to my mountain had grown up over the past twenty years with innumerable small trees rooted in huge ruts. I did not even try to navigate it. Instead, I would park my motorcycle over at Sassafras, load up a backpack, and transfer a few items from one mountain to the other on foot.

I felt weak. I moved slowly. I had to stop often to regain my strength and balance. I wanted only to get to a safe space, to set up my pup tent and live by the fire and use the life water from a spring nearby to cleanse my body and soothe my Spirit.

I sensed something on this land. I felt that She had been lonely. Although it was late spring, the Earth still slept. I heard few birds and saw only a few small animals about at first. Somehow, I understood our Mother Earth as a living being. She had been awaiting my arrival. Cared for and honored and acknowledged, She would come alive. I knew this to be so. And so it was: The birds and butterflies as Her jewelry, the flowers as Her perfume, they all began to return, shyly that first season, and boldly in later years, when the beavers, coyotes, foxes, wolves, bears, deer, elk, wild turkeys, and owls filled the woods, and eagles soared above.

I walked back and forth, back and forth, up and down the mountain, along the bluffs and gorges, through dense forest and newer regrowth arising in the wake of sloppy logging work. I wore moccasins to stay connected through touch with our Mother Earth, gathering Her power into my soul. Many hours I stayed here in the clearing, praying and crying, trying to understand the vision I had received. I asked the Spirits and my Ancestors, *What am I supposed to do now that I am here? How am I supposed to do this?*

Soon after my arrival on the land, a friend brought Jenny back to me from Dallas. For some months, we lived alone on our mountain, mother and daughter reunited.

We rose with the sun, gathered firewood, and collected water. We built a little lean-to out of trees for a kitchen, with a counter for our pots and pans. I would make our food with grain, basic rations like oatmeal, potatoes and onions and carrots, rice and beans—things that were easy to tend. We cooked them over the fire. In the afternoons, we scrambled down to the creek to swim and relax. At night, we cuddled right up against each other in the tent, telling stories and talking of our adventures of the day, the plants and rocks and animals we had met, our plans for the next morning.

We were both like children, absorbing what we saw, learning about our mountain. I had already started learning about medicinal herbs before I left the city. Now I began identifying the herbs growing around me and using them appropriately. I had brought two books out to the land: Jethro Kloss's *Back to Eden* and Alma Hutchens's *Indian Herbalogy of North America*. Those were my two bibles. They didn't have photos, just drawings and descriptions of the herbs' properties and purposes. That is how I began using herbs, just in that way. I studied the knowledge other people had gathered and put into books, and I sensed the Earth around me.

Soon the whispers of the trees, the intuitive voices of the plants, began to make sense to me. I learned their language. I began to learn how to honor the medicine, the herbs, the environment. By osmosis, it seemed, I began to understand. Through my being, I absorbed old understandings, like a remembering.

As Swami Muktananda had told me—and many wise elders would repeat in the years to come—in the attainment of enlightenment you must have a vision, something you want, a desire you burn to fulfill. I wanted guidance. I cried and prayed for it, by day and by night. I opened myself to the Spirits for direction. *Please tell me what to do*, I begged. Then I waited.

One day, as Jenny and I made the trek from Sassafras to Arco Iris, I felt the presence of another being. Looking up, I noticed within clear vision of the same high path I had traveled many times already, an astonishing sight: Jutting out of a south-facing rocky bluff, pushing up through massive boulders, a gnarled and knotted old cedar tree stood alone, alive against all odds. How could I not have noticed Her before, this ancient being who appeared to spring from stone, not soil, Her very existence in this spot a miracle? *Please send me a teacher, an elder, to show me the way. I need a guide, someone who has been here and done this before. Muéstrame el camino, por favor*, I had begged. We had not been alone after all. Grandmother Cedar had been watching our efforts. *Have faith*, She now said. *Be patient.* There

She stood, speaking through Her body and being every lesson of survival we would need, as we too put down roots in the face of adversity. *Alone on a rocky path,* Her being said, *you must be resourceful, determined, and constant.*

I fell to my knees before Her in gratitude and awe. That very day, I created an altar there, where in the years and decades to come—to this day— I would return with *ofrendas* of copal, tobacco, and flowers, or sometimes money, or gifts from my travels, such as sea sponge gathered in Florida. I would bring compost and spring water to supplement Her meager diet. I would come to pray, to cry, to shed my concerns, to seek Her counsel. She would drop small, green cedar boughs as gifts for me. Once She offered me a broken limb, which became my Ceremonial Talking Stick for decades. Sacred and steady, Abuelita Cedro has always guided me gently back onto the Red Road, toward Arco Iris, our Rainbow Land.

♪ ♪ ♪

I needed a clearer path to our land. Bringing our provisions by motorcycle from Fayetteville to Sassafras; loading myself, Jenny, and our dog with canvas sacks of varying weights; and journeying across the gorge, across the creek, and up another mountain to Arco Iris took all my strength. Sometimes it took more strength than little Jenny had; we had to stop often to let her rest. During the rainy seasons, the creek became a raging river. In winter it would be impassable. I feared the onset of cold weather before we had built a tipi, secured enough firewood, and stocked enough provisions.

Thinking strategically, I traded my motorcycle for a little truck, straight across. The truck could make it from Fayetteville to the foot of our mountain loaded with more stuff than I could bring on ten motorcycle runs. Then I got a couple of ponies, pack horses—Welsh mix, small and stocky. I sewed canvas bags for the horses, filled these with our goods, secured Jenny on a horse straddling some bags, and led the ponies back up to our camp, leaving the truck at the bottom of the road on the side of the highway, near the church in Boxley.

We started coming up the overgrown logging road that way. I remember one time walking Jenny and two ponies up the road. I kept turning back to look at her because she was falling asleep. I was afraid she would slide off. I felt through my moccasins something move under my foot. I looked down to see a giant rattlesnake stretched across the road, almost as long as the road was wide. I had stepped across its midsection with the arch of my foot. Well, I just kept walking, and it just kept going the direction it was going, crossing the road. We made a little T there, and nothing happened. I felt protected and unafraid. I did not scream or run or do anything. I stayed on my path.

Nothing about the mountain, the earth, the plants and animals, or the wind and sky and elements frightened me. Jenny and I listened and learned from these good neighbors how to live in harmony. We took only what we needed, always with gratitude. We foraged. We planted our first garden, digging by hand through the rocky clay soil to prepare it for planting. We used the large boulders we removed to landscape our herb and flower beds. We witnessed the beauty that came forth, by magic, from our Mother's womb.

❦ ❦ ❦

Men created hazards. Loggers with chainsaws polluted the sounds of nature for miles around. And hunters came back here, truckloads of them. Nobody had been living on this side of the mountains, on these prime hunting grounds, for decades. Men with guns punctured our peace, white men with guns, drinking men with guns. I had to teach my little girl how to run and hide, how to blend into the environment, dodge behind a boulder, align herself with the trunk of a thick tree. I kept no guns, not after Joe's murder. I would not allow them on the land for many years.

When we first got here, and for a long time after, the locals put out the unwelcome mat. Sassafras already had a reputation as a crazy hippie commune—and that was a white community. Since I had to go through Sassafras to get to my home at first, the neighbors took me for a Sassafras woman. That did not help as an introduction.

Then word started getting out that an Indian woman had taken up residence on the mountain with her little girl. The whole Boxley Valley community—a very small circle of white people who consider themselves the "natives," the original homesteaders of the area from Boxley to Ponca and up Cave Mountain—knew we were there. They knew they did not like us, long before they ever said a word to us. Those families owned the land in Newton County. They sat as county judges and wore the sheriffs' badges. They attended the Boxley Baptist Church, which just happened to be at the foot of my mountain. From the parsonage, the preacher and his wife peeked out from behind curtains to watch my comings and goings. They knew I did not go anywhere on Sunday mornings, which made me a pagan or a witch, for starters, I later learned.

Because we were so poor, Jenny and I, we often had problems. Our truck would break down or get stuck in the mud. At first, I thought we could go to the nearest farmhouse and ask to use the phone, call for a tow truck or for a friend to come. But the locals would not answer the door. In any weather conditions—cold, wet, stormy—they would not answer the door. I could see their cars parked in the drive. I could hear them inside. So we would walk a mile down to the store, where they would hurry to lock the door and put up their "closed" sign. Next, we would walk down to the home of Yoldeen, the postal lady; no one home there. Then I would turn in the other direction, dragging this frozen little kid all over the place. Same thing at the parsonage. Understood. We got it. We were not welcome.

Jenny and I lived in solitude on the mountain. Except on the occasional trip into Fayetteville for provisions, we interacted with no other people.

Then one day I heard human footsteps crackling through the brush, and our lives changed again.

8

This Land Is Our Land

The waning sun made a halo of her curls as she approached our encampment, an overstuffed pack on her back.

"Shiner."

"Please let me stay, SunHawk. I know you're SunHawk now, and you have no reason to take me back. I ran like a coward."

Jenny peeked out of the pup tent, into which I had pushed her at the sound of human footsteps approaching. She slipped silently into Shiner's arms, pulling in as close as one being could to another.

I took a deep breath and a long step forward, heart leading head, until my arms cradled them both. With my face immersed in Shiner's dark nest of regrown ringlets and my shoulders heaving, I could not speak.

"I beg you to forgive me. I won't do it again. I love you, SunHawk. I love Jenny. I'll stay this time, and always. If you allow it."

"We can try it" was all I said.

Shiner started doing the town runs in her little car. I stayed back on the land, where I wanted to be, sewing the white canvas panels gifted to me by Berry for a tipi. With that task completed, we gathered poles for the dwelling's structure. Then Shiner, Jenny, and I moved from the pup tent to the tipi, our first real home at Arco Iris.

Soon Leona Garcia moved out to the land with us. Occasionally other women of color we had known in Dallas or Austin or Fayetteville would pass through. Some brought children with them. Word traveled in the various communities we touched—Latina, Indigenous, Black, lesbian, alternative. A number of poor white mothers found their way to us, too, some with their biracial children and some simply because Newton County had no shelter for battered women at that time; word spread that we offered refuge. Somehow, and slowly at first, women began to hear that they could find sanctuary with us, and they drifted in and out. Some of these women traveled around to women's lands across the country, staying a while and then moving on. We learned some valuable skills from these travelers, seasoned outdoorswomen used to living frugally and resourcefully.

I still struggled to understand how to carry out what my ongoing visions told me to do, with nothing but woods here, no infrastructure at all. How was I to provide refuge? What did that mean, when we were squatting—with permission—on land owned by Diana Rivers and the Sassafras collective? I prayed about it, cried about it, prayed some more. I asked for direction, and then I just went about my life. Here we lived simply, tending the fire, fetching the water, gathering and growing and preparing the food over the open fire, all very close to our Mother Earth.

Finally the Spirits of the Land and the Ancestors spoke to me. *Remember the Sacredness of our original ways.* We needed autonomy. Complete autonomy. To be self-empowered, to feel that empowerment, we needed to secure the land for ourselves, for our vision, for our mission. We could not remain dependent on the goodwill of the Sassafras women. Diana had said when I came over here that she would help put in some water, help fix the road. I had waited, hoping for her to come through. The time of waiting had to end. *Become a Warrior of the Land. Teach the women and children who come to be Rainbow Warriors.*

Although I still remained physically weak and fragile at that time, I felt the Spirits of the Land, the Warriors of the Land, the Ancestors of this land around me. I called them all. *You must all go with me, be with me. Bring me my Warrior energy.*

Shiner, still a member of the Sassafras collective, went with me for an arranged meeting with the four other members who remained on the land. We drove up to the main gate to find the other Sassafras women about to leave on a beer run, apparently forgetting our meeting time. Their nonchalance saddened me. I told them calmly that I needed to meet with them for a brief time, if they could wait.

We met in a circle. I voiced what we needed as Indigenous women and Indigenous peoples: We needed autonomy on our own land, land that had been stolen from us hundreds of years ago, in order to regain our power, our self-identity, to reclaim ourselves in our way of life. We needed to have our land be *our land*—in our names, with no one dictating how we lived.

Four of the collective members, including Shiner, agreed quickly. Those others probably wanted to get on with their beer run. Diana voted no. I do not recall that she gave any reason. If she objected to being so fully out-voted because she was the original owner of the land and older by about two decades than the rest of us, she nonetheless conceded. Luckily for us, Sassafras operated on simple majority, not consensus.

"I'll have my lawyer draw the deed," she said.

We agreed that the land would be privately owned by me and Leona Garcia, the two women of color then living there. One hundred twenty acres, separated from the Sassafras land by the natural boundary of Beech Creek.

We were twenty-three years old, Leona and I. What did we know? We had little conception of land ownership as a legal or financial exchange. We wanted to take the sacred land out of their hands. Our land should be our responsibility. And nobody should be able to tell us to leave it, ever again.

For a year I waited for Diana to bring me a deed. I kept asking her about it. "I'm waiting for my lawyer in New York to get back to me," she would say.

She met me in Fayetteville, flustered and rushing to catch a flight. "I have it, I have it," she said. "I just need you to sign it right now, and I'll take it to New York."

I looked at the sheaf of paper she thrust at me, a long paper trail with a lot of legal jargon. I tried to stay calm as I leafed through it. It had our names on it, but I could not understand much else written there.

"Here's a pen," Diana urged.

Spirit told me not to sign it.

"No," I said. "I won't be signing this right now. I have to keep it, so I can get somebody to help me understand it."

Very reluctantly, Diana left empty-handed, as I held the document high in my hand.

The next day, I went to the free legal clinic in Fayetteville, asking them to look it over for me. When they called me back in the next week, they said, "This deed would not hold up in court. She could use anything to invalidate this deed." They showed me where it said that the land would be returned to the original owner, among other loopholes. They said, "We can draw you up a deed with all the specs that are on here. We have everything we need, and we'll draw you up one." And so they did.

When Diana returned from Upstate New York, I literally threw her deed back at her. "I'm not signing that," I said. "This is just the same old shit y'all have done to our people for hundreds of years. Phony treaties, phony deeds." I held up my new document for her to see; I was not going to entrust the authority to her again. "I'm going to do this myself," I said. "I'm going to get the collective members' signatures for this real deed, which my lawyers drew up, and you can sign it."

I went around over the next few days to each one of the members and got them to sign off. Then I took the deed to the courthouse in Jasper and got it filed. Diana signed it all right. She had been overruled. She had tried to get around it. Nobody would have known had Spirit not guided me to get legal help.

It took a year from my arrival on the land to complete the legal transfer. After that, Diana and I became archenemies. I did not trust her at all. I had good reason not to trust her.

I will never know if she actively promoted the rumor that I had stolen the land—a rumor that spread like wildfire among the white lesbian and white upper-class alternative communities of Northwest Arkansas and beyond—or if she simply chose not to squelch it. Dousing that fire when it first flared could have spared us decades of hardship and alienation from potential allies in the region. I knew the truth all along. I believe Diana did too.

9

Drama in These Hills

The white old-timers in the Ozarks called our sacred ancient mountains "hills," and if these hills could speak, the locals would have glued their ears to the ground night and day. They wanted like nobody's business to get into our business, as their imaginations ran wild about us: pagans, devil's spawn, drug addicts, "unnatural" women.

For a brief time, we sent Jenny to public school in the county. We trekked three miles down the road to catch the school bus, then three miles back at the end of the school day. The bus driver taunted her as much as the kids did: Your mother's an Indian. Your mother's a lesbian. Your mother's a pagan. Not so far off. Of course I would not subject Jenny to the very evils we had left the city to escape. We decided to homeschool her. Shiner's parents sent books, while Mother Earth became Jenny's open-air school and playground.

Diana reneged on the help she had offered previously to upgrade our road. It took us two years to save the money to make it even marginally passable. I found a fellow named Billy Clark, who lived over toward Kingston. He agreed to hire a bulldozer and help us open the road. Others did not want our money. Folks said Billy was mixed-blood, part Indian. Maybe that's why he talked to us.

With the road opened up, hunters started coming further back into our place. They drove all the way back here, parking on our land, going all around us shooting wildlife. I told them this was private property; we did not want any hunting over here—no trespassing. I even put up signs. The men told me straight out, "We've been hunting these parts all our lives and always will."

We had to teach all the women and children who passed through Rainbow Land to stay together, to hide behind boulders, to run, to visualize exit plans. The sounds of the vehicles alerted us to outsiders' presence as we walked the three miles up the road to our home. We could conceal ourselves until they passed. Sometimes they did not come that far and we could slip quietly through the woods.

The preacher confronted us one day. He and his deacons wanted to pay us a visit. "We need to see what y'all are doing up there." I told him absolutely not. After that, they started harassing us about parking our vehicle down by the old schoolhouse, which did not even belong to the Boxley Baptist Church at that time. We kept right on parking there, until we got the road opened all the way to our land. The preacher and his wife kept on watching us: women and children, people of color, making our way up the mountain, disappearing into the woods for weeks at a time.

Our occasional encounters on the road fueled the locals' nightmares. I had taken to wearing a headband and moccasins, as had several others at both Arco Iris and Sassafras. We all wore belts with buck knives attached. The men out there did, and as we said back then, "If the men can fucking do it, we can too." Out on the road, we usually carried machetes as well, to clear the trail along the way—not to mention their deterrent effect. I don't think anyone took us for damsels in distress.

In the warm weather, we often went topless, with our shirts tucked into our belts in case we heard a truck coming along. Further back here on the land, we would wear only a breechcloth in the summer, a tiny wrap, enough to cover the bush and no more. Without washing machines, we had to wash our stuff in the creek and hang it up to dry. The less to keep clean, the better.

I will never forget the day that Jenny and I made our way over to Sassafras on some errands, through the woods to the gorge and up the Cave Mountain side, all on women's land, in our skimpy summer attire. In fact, I had removed even my breechcloth for a moment to wash it out in case any ticks had found a sweet spot there. I stood completely naked, except for moccasins and belt with buck knife, when I heard a loud, gravelly voice call out, "I have never, ever seen straight hair down there."

I looked out to the clearing to see this tiny, beautiful Black goddess of a woman, with glowing nut-brown skin and beaded braids streaming down her back. Isis. Queen Isis.

She had just arrived at Sassafras, one of many women who passed through during the warm weather. Some stayed a week in Arkansas. Some stayed a year or two. Isis, it turned out, would stay a lifetime.

Unlike most of the women I encountered at Sassafras in the early years, Isis expressed active interest in Rainbow Land. She wanted to know what we were doing to make a difference for women of color. "Are you political?" she would ask. "You need radical politics to change the system. Not just talk. Blah. Blah. Blah." That was her polite version. Isis said anything to anyone. Even before her daughter Princess died, she had few filters; after, she just did not give a damn.

Like all of us, Isis had her contradictions. Raised in DC, she felt drawn to the rural. Mouthy and street tough, she had a college education. Trained in ballet, she had also strutted the runway of a strip joint or two along the way. Still married to a man, she swung hard into radical lesbian feminism. She was figuring herself out.

Born Sheila Elaine Brown, "Isis" came to Arkansas as a self-styled radical. She had been a member of the Yvonne Wanrow Defense Committee, fighting to free the American Indian woman who had been convicted of second-degree murder for killing the known child molester who threatened her son and nephew. Then the summer of 1977 brought Isis to the Traditional Elders and Youth Circle, where Phillip Deere and other tribal leaders fired her up about Indigenous cultures and people, whose blood she also shared. She headed toward battle as a way of life.

At the same time, Isis fought inner demons, which flitted in and out of her mind. Weed calmed her; she smoked a lot of it. Then she talked and talked, and she had stories to tell. Many people, women and men, liked to party with her over the years. They reeled at the spectacle of a human being who would speak any thought that came into her head, including strong medicine for the person standing in front of her.

She began a cycle of stays at Sassafras, broken up by a few days here and there at Arco Iris, trips to DC to earn some cash and see Princess, and stops at women's peace encampments and other protest actions around the nation. Isis also worked the Michigan Womyn's Music Festival, which was held every summer from 1976 on. As a member of the "long crew," she spent nearly a month each summer helping to set up and tear down the festival in rural Michigan. Somehow Isis managed to make friends wherever she went, even as she called out everyone's bullshit every chance she got.

And there was a lot of bullshit going on at Sassafras. Lesbian separatism seemed like the only thing the women over there agreed on.

Although the seven white women of the collective owned the land there as coequals, in reality Diana Rivers pretty much called the shots. She had all the money. At first only white women stayed out there, a working-class group and an upper-class group. They had constant battles among themselves over how to use the land and who could use the land and who could make decisions. Then to complicate things even more, they decided to invite some "multicultural" women out. They put up announcements at the women's music festivals and in various feminist magazines and newsletters: "Lesbian land, looking to diversify. Welcome!"

They caught Buffy and Clary first. Buffy came from Upstate New York and was part Native American, part white. Clary came from Panama originally. Those two invited their friends from the West Coast and New York, until Sassafras, in the middle of the all-white Arkansas Ozarks, had a pretty sizeable group of women of color on that one land, all in different little cabins and huts.

Meanwhile we lived over here on women-of-color land. We were Two-Spirited. We continued to take care of children who needed a home. Sometimes lesbians' kids, sometimes not. Even human services brought kids to us, though we did not have much to live on. We kept a no alcohol, no drug abuse, no guns policy. We respected our Mother Earth. We did not bow to people who happened to have money. We had two separate ways of life on the two mountains.

I tried to be in a good way with them over there, not ruffle feathers as I walked through to pick up my motorcycle. With Shiner still in the Sassafras collective, though, I could not help hearing about their battles. Constant battles. Constant meetings. Diana and the others would not put any of the women of color in the governing body of the collective. Whatever the white women claimed as their politics, this stayed the reality. It came to blows many times.

I even got in the middle of it one time. The white women had been sharing a land truck amongst themselves. When the women of color came with little city cars that proved useless for hauling stuff back into the woods on those rough roads, the white women found endless excuses not to share the truck, leaving the women of color more or less stranded back there on the land.

One day, Jenny, Shiner, and I—my little clan—went over to Sassafras for a birthday party with the women of color residing there. When I saw the truck sitting there, my anger flared. I yanked up the hood and pulled a plug off the distributor cap, on the backside where you couldn't see. Then I left a note on the windshield: "Until y'all can share this truck, nobody's using it." I signed it, and we went on to the party.

We had a good time. Then, driving off, we found the road blocked by another truck, occupied by Diana and her henchwomen. Briar—probably the tallest and strongest woman I have ever seen, a mechanic, and the one who had run off with Shiner when I lay dying—got out on the passenger side and went to open my hood.

"What the hell are you doing?" I yelled.

"Dismantling your truck!"

"Oh yeah? Try it!" I jumped out of the truck.

Briar got me by the throat, up against the radiator, backing me up, pinning me, strangling me, as I tried to angle my blade out of its sheath.

Next thing I knew, Shiner took a running jump onto Briar's back, grabbing her around the neck, until the two of them tumbled into the dirt and Briar rolled out of reach before I could stab her.

It could have gotten horrible before we cooled off and went our separate ways.

These mountains have harbored some women's drama. I see it now: Everyone sought sanctuary. Everyone sought a safe space, to escape being shunned or beaten or killed for being ourselves. That's what lesbian women faced in the cities. Native American communities did not always offer refuge for Two-Spirit women either. The lesbian separatists felt they had to swing hard into the matriarchal, into expressions of power. They had to be strong in their convictions. They had to dig the pain and oppression out of themselves. I understand what they had to process. In the meantime, they were being asses. I see that now.

Even Diana, I believe, did want the best for the land, as much as she was aware and awake. In time, we would bury the hatchet, in solemn and sacred Ceremony.

10

Growing *La Familia*

One summer, we got word that Shiner's grandmother was dying up in Minnesota.

"Let's go see her on the way back from Michigan," I said. "You should at least go say goodbye."

When we got to Minneapolis, we found Frances Friedman Cardozo strapped to her wheelchair in a pricey nursing home, convinced that the Nazis had her marked for extermination. Mostly nonverbal and overtaken by dementia, she remained physically robust at the age of eighty-two. She just wanted out of there.

"Maybe we should take her home with us." I was always the one to think of these crazy things.

"How, SunHawk?"

"We'll get a trailer, an RV." We had opened the road at that point; we could pull a trailer up there attached to my truck. "She shouldn't live her life out this way." They had her drugged as well as restrained. But that old lady had a lot of life in her. I could feel it.

We called Shiner's parents in San Francisco to discuss the plan. They rejected it.

"Give them a day," Shiner said.

Sure enough, the next day they called with a counter plan: "We will rent an apartment for you in Minneapolis. For a year. We'll pay you to take care of Grandma what we were paying the nursing home. Show us you can be responsible and then you can bring her to Arkansas."

We found an apartment on the side of town with a large Indian population, several different tribes. With Shiner taking care of Frannie and Jenny going to a diverse public school with lots of Indian and Mexican and Black and Vietnamese kids, I had time on my hands. Wanting to get involved in the local Indigenous community, I headed over to the nearby Native American center to check out their programs and activities.

"Indian Homes for Indian Children," the woman told me. "That's the program with the most desperate need."

Next thing we knew, we had two little malnourished girls living with us. Lila and Kelly, ages one and a half and three. Their mom had been abusing alcohol and drugs. She had left the children in their apartment unattended for a couple of days when the authorities swooped in and took them from her. Indian Homes for Indian Children worked to reunite families by getting parents help while keeping their children from being displaced into the white world.

In pretty quick order, we got the girls all fat and cute. Shiny black hair. Coal-dark eyes. They ran open-armed around the apartment, hugging and laughing and climbing on laps. When Frannie vaguely batted them away, in her dementia, they came right back at her, full of love and energy. Even the old lady gave in to their affection.

We settled in to a Minneapolis winter, which was much colder than anything I had ever experienced or wanted to experience again. Then after nine months, with everyone thriving, I decided that Shiner's parents needed to get off the pot. We all needed to go home to our sacred land. As good as it was to be living in a diverse community in Minneapolis, the impoverishment of the neighborhood—with bars and liquor stores and pawn shops and pool halls broadcasting what colonization does to a people—saddened me. We had more than proved to the Cardozos that we were capable of caring for their elder, I felt. Could we take Frannie to Arkansas or not? So they bought an RV, a sixteen-footer, and released us on back to our mountain.

✒ ✒ ✒

Kelly and Lila's mom, Robyn, had been coming to see the girls on regular visits. We developed a relationship with her after her initial, understandable distrust. We bonded deeply with her children. She could not take them back yet, because she had to do her rehab program for a full year.

I told her, "We're going to be leaving soon. I want you to know." Then we sat, one mother and another, for a while.

She said, "My sister can take Lila until I'm out of the program. She can't take them both. Please take Kelly with you. She has made a strong bond with you. I know you'll take good care of her. And when I get situated, I'll come get her."

That is where we left it. We both knew we had cut a renegade deal. I had been designated a temporary guardian; the state had custody. I knew that the state would never grant us custody as a lesbian couple. Robyn distrusted the government even more than I did. We made an agreement one Indian woman to another. We exchanged contact information. Before we left town, she also provided me with a handwritten and notarized letter giving me permission to bring Kelly to Arkansas. Robyn knew where to find me when she was ready. Kelly returned to Arkansas with us and her mother's blessing.

On the mountain, we resumed our lives, not without a few hiccups. We had to readjust to fetching water from a spring, cooking over an open fire, and living in relative isolation from other human beings. Jenny at first missed her schoolmates. Kelly missed her little sister and mom. And yet, the absolute, full-bodied joy Kelly expressed as she discovered the animals and plants, the rocks and soil, the clear sunshine and starry night sky, and most especially, the mountain spring, whose water she loved to play in—this joy more than made up for the bumps. We had come home!

I moved back into the tipi with Jenny and Kelly. Shiner moved into the RV with her grandmother, to keep an eye on her at night. It had everything: a heater, a stove, and a refrigerator, all propane.

While we could take adequate care of Frannie in the trailer, we could not take optimal care of her there. Carrying her out from the RV down rickety little metal steps to put her in the wheelchair out in the yard did not amount to real mobility for her. I wanted to do better. For that we needed a house.

I started going to the library for books on how to build a house. The only structure I had ever built up to that point was a small, outdoor lean-to kitchen. So I started drawing up plans, envisioning a twenty-by-seventy-foot lean-to design with a shed-style roof. Then we began gathering materials wherever we could find them: green lumber, used windows and doors, stuff we could get free or cheap to make the shell.

Mom and Dad visited from Texas, bringing food, provisions, clothes, blankets, even our first generator. They camped in a big family tent. As former migrant workers, they knew how to rough it. Mom cooked over the open fire, while Dad surveyed the land and offered advice. Shiner's parents contributed $5,000 toward house construction, and John Cardozo, Shiner's Harvard-educated dad, came up to witness the groundbreaking, too.

🪶 🪶 🪶

I continued to learn about the edible plants and herbs growing wild on the land. We also extended our garden. Before long, we could grow or gather a good portion of our food, stretching our bounty through the winter by canning, drying, and stocking our pantry.

I spent countless hours walking the mountain, up and down, across and around. I grew to know the communities of trees and plants, as they grew to know me. They cleared walking paths for me gradually. I stepped lightly among them, speaking, sometimes chanting or singing, my gratitude for their generosity. I never took more than I needed from an individual family of plants. I snapped a few leaves here, pulled a few roots there, to prepare my growing array of medicinal salves and tinctures, teas and tonics, and to fill our bellies. Herbs and edibles, berries and flowers, bark and seed, root and stem. As much as I learned from books and from teachers across the planet, I learned the most from Mother Earth herself, on my own mountain.

Over the years, I would learn from the lore of both Indigenous peoples and local hill people that many plants had migrated to the Ozarks during the Ice Age and survived. For centuries, spiritual people from all over North America had come here to gather healing medicine and do Ceremony on this neutral ground, owned by no one, open to all. *Tlatzokamati.*

🪶 🪶 🪶

The locals remained hostile to us. When we entered places of business, silence descended. We got in and out as fast as we could, avoiding confrontation.

Only Isis enjoyed messing with people. She would go right up to them. "How you doing?" she'd say, as they tried to peer through her.

I recall an incident at the grocery store in Jasper. Leona and I stood on one end of the produce section, Isis on the other, when an old white woman nearly ran over me with her cart. Jaw hanging, eyes popping, she pointed at Isis, "Is that a colored lady over there?"

"Isis," I called out, "are you a colored lady?"

"Some people call me that. I'm Black," she said as the white woman fled the scene.

Another time, a few of us ran into the preacher from Shiloh at the grocery store. He yelled over from the next checkout line, "Is it true that you'ns shot down a crop duster that was flying over y'all's property?" Of course we never did that. Locals who are now friends of mine have told me folks believed that we not only hated men but also had man-eating dogs. At best, they had us pegged as witches.

Sometimes things got scary, like the day a pile of rednecks in a pickup tried to run Leona and me into a ditch as we walked along the shoulder of a blacktop road in Huntsville, where we had gone to do laundry. "Dirty Indians!" Their tires splattered mud across our bright panchos. I prayed for a circle of protection around us.

One frigid winter day, Shiner and I loaded five kids into the unheated camper top of our truck to make the trek from Fayetteville to the land. We had gone into town to fetch little Tara, Tito, and Harold, whose mom, Belle, a single Black lesbian friend of ours, needed some childcare over the weekend while she worked. Kelly and Jenny made five. All bundled in blankets, they played on the camper mattress as we wound our way through the back roads and small towns we knew well by reputation if nothing else.

Although we knew to avoid Huntsville when we could, we decided to stop at the Amber Light Inn and Café for some hot cocoa to warm the kids up. Six people of color, plus Shiner, we walked into the one-room diner, all of two booths and four tables, to await seating. The place went dead silent. No one came forward to seat us. So we seated ourselves and waited for the waitress, who had already served the few other customers. We waited, kids quiet, for about fifteen minutes. No service.

I said to Shiner, as I did in these situations where she had more privilege, "Go talk to those people. Tell them we just want some cocoa for the kids and coffee for us." She did it. Then we waited for another fifteen minutes. No service.

Finally, not wanting to risk a fight with the kids present, we gathered them, all warm and toasty now, back into the truck for the second half of our journey. We had barely peeled out from the Amber Light Inn when we noticed a cop car following us. After ten miles or so, right as we approached the Madison County line, the blue lights flicked on to pull us over.

"I'll need to see your license." It was none other than Sheriff Ralph Baker, known to us as a corrupt, racist son of a bitch. In Fayetteville, I had heard Black women in particular speak of his reputation for violence. Baker would later die mysteriously, in a swirl of allegations including drug trafficking and murder.

"What's wrong?" I asked. "Do I have a headlight out? What's the problem?"

"You left without paying your bill. You're going back to pay it."

I felt a familiar rage rising in me. We had a carload of cold children, and we could not get served at the inn. "Is this all you have the time to do, hunt down women and children who haven't done anything wrong? We didn't get anything there. They did not serve us."

"You ordered something and you didn't pay for it. You're going back and you're going to pay." Shiner clutched my arm so hard she almost punctured my skin, trying to keep me quiet. Baker leaned close in. He said, "You better shut up or you're going to find yourself face-down in a four-by-eight cell."

We drove all the way back to the inn with the sheriff on our tail. I walked back into the café, threw some money on the counter, and turned to leave.

"You forgot your change," Baker said, grabbing me and shoving it into my hand.

I tossed the coins over my shoulder at him as I sauntered off in my work boots, tipping my cowboy hat at the wide-eyed little waitress who had refused to serve us.

Let's just say that whenever possible, we tried to drive straight through to Fayetteville.

✶ ✶ ✶

In those early years on the land, we lived close to our Mother Earth, surrounded by nature, all of us trying to survive each day, to retreat, to heal, to remove ourselves from the traumas of our past, to forge futures for ourselves and our children. We still walked up an almost impossible three-mile dirt road, lived in tents and tipis, hauled water from the spring by hand, and cooked our food over an open fire.

As word spread, we did more and more collective child-rearing. The separatists at Sassafras began to call me the Pied Piper. Women would come here, then need to go away to figure themselves out. They would leave the kids here. We made room. One woman, a mixed-blood who traveled from one women's land settlement to another, left her little boy, Micah, with us for a few months. Burning Cloud brought a little Native American boy all the way from the Northwest to stay with us for a while. A white lesbian we knew left her three biracial children with us for a whole summer. We gave her a break until she could get herself together. Many times, when the Newton County women's shelter, or the one in Harrison, filled up, women in crisis found their way to us to ask for help and housing. We always found a place for them, as the river of women and children kept flowing in our direction.

Shiner and I were living here with Frannie, Kelly, and Jenny when two young, beautiful women came out to the land seeking sanctuary. One was Apache and the other, her girlfriend, was white—and Jewish. They arrived with a little U-Haul trailer, California plates. We didn't ask too many questions. We let them stay in a tiny cabin, a one-room shack down the hill from our encampment, after explaining clearly our no guns, no alcohol, no hard drugs policy.

They seemed laid back and friendly, willing to put in sweat equity gardening, chopping wood, and helping to clear the road. We hung out at night with them around the fire pit, under the stars. Nothing about them seemed different from other lesbians we knew in those days who had taken to the road, stopping at one women's land community or another, seeking sisterhood and liberation. We even let them plant a few—six, to be exact—pot plants in our garden, where the brushy overgrowth of many vegetable varieties gave the forbidden weed cover. While we did not smoke marijuana, we saw no harm in letting these women keep their plants growing during their stay on the land.

The U-Haul trailer bothered me. They had no intention of returning it, they told me. "You can't leave it sitting here like that," I said. "We could get in trouble if the law comes out here for any reason. Stolen property." So they painted it green, to cover up the U-Haul logo. I still felt uneasy.

Then one day they drove their car into town, leaving the trailer on the land. When they had not returned after a week, I decided to go down to the cabin to check out what they had left behind. I just got a vibe about it. Guns. I found guns in the cabin, and more guns in the unlocked trailer, among other possessions they would be sure to miss: Indian blankets and drums, a tipi and other artifacts.

Shiner and I went to Fayetteville looking for them. The food co-op, now lesbian-run, seemed a logical place to ask about these women. No surprise, they had passed through, in the company of a quiet young white man from St. Louis or Kansas City or somewhere. He seemed to be a high-volume dealer, moving many kilos of pot between states. Oh, and the Apache woman had apparently escaped from prison somewhere in California or New Mexico.

A few weeks later, a couple of lesbians from Fayetteville showed up at Rainbow Land. "Y'all need to know: The Feds are after those women. That guy has gone missing. Last seen with them. The Feds have been asking all kinds of questions about y'all. They'll be coming out here soon."

Shiner and I raced to stash their belongings deep in the woods. We camo'd everything, especially the guns, and not a moment too soon. Federal agents bumped their way up the mountain to interrogate us. They spread out over our settlement, searching inch by inch for something. "He had a white van," they told us. "We need to locate it." We told them honestly that we had never seen a white van or white man connected to those women. They flew a search plane overhead, too. Seems that the missing guy had some very rich, politically connected parents who wanted to know why their son had not made it home.

Years later, I ran into the white woman in San Francisco. I confronted her. Why would they bring that heat on us? She broke down even then, unable to say more than a few words. Apparently, she had helped her lover escape from prison. They ran for the hills. Just happened to be my hill. She did not think that young hippie guy ever made it back home alive.

🪶🪶🪶

Shortly after the Feds came up here, we made our annual trip to the Michigan Womyn's Music Festival, where we could pull in enough money selling the herbal medicines I had begun to make—along with homemade quilts, nachos, popcorn, whatever we could prepare and sell—to help sustain us through the year.

One day, a brown-skinned, short-haired Latina stopped by our stall. She began peppering me with questions.

"Hold it," I told her. "I don't have time to talk unless you work with me."

She washed her hands and got inside the stall to cook up nachos with me. All the while, questions poured out. She was Luisa Cruz, lifelong New Yorker with a dream of living on women's land.

I doubted she could be of much use in the wilderness. "What do you know how to do?"

"I renovate apartments, in the city." She participated in a program that trained women in carpentry.

"I could really use a carpenter," I told her. "I'm designing and building a house, a double-envelope 'echo' house. One frame and then another, two buildings inside of one. A foot thick and very well insulated. Think you could handle that?"

"No problem." She had her thumbs hooked in her pant pockets, boots planted wide apart, eye contact constant, almost challenging. Very butch. She stood just a couple of inches shorter than me. Charisma and muscles made up the gap.

"I can't pay you," I said. "If you want to move there, live there, I can give you a place to stay. Food. But I can't pay you."

About a year later Luisa arrived on a Greyhound bus from New York.

Soon after our return to Arkansas from Michigan, the local sheriff and his two deputies showed up on our land, in camo and fully armed, with a warrant to search. They had been alerted by the Feds that we had a stolen, out-of-state U-Haul trailer up here, and during our absence had come up to poke around. They were looking for anything they could find.

"The U-Haul is not mine," I told them when they tried to bust me for stealing it. They confiscated it.

Next they started stomping around our garden. "You've got marijuana plants in here," the sheriff said.

"That is not true," I countered. We had remembered the six plants while in Michigan and pulled them up the minute we got home. I hung the plants up to dry in the loft of the little cabin where the two outlaw women had stayed.

While the heavily armed white men crashed through our vegetable garden with increasing agitation, Jenny slipped away. The men noticed. "Hey, there was another little girl here! Where'd she go? We aim to arrest all y'all for possession of marijuana."

They handcuffed me and marched me down the road to the cabin, the only structure on the premises other than our tipi and Frannie's RV, which they had already searched. One of the deputies stayed back with the rest of the suspects: an old lady with dementia in a wheelchair, Shiner, and little Kelly.

Jenny could not have been more than nine years old at the time. But we kept no secrets from her. She knew we could get in trouble for the pot plants, and she knew we had carried them down to the cabin both to hang them up to dry and to hide them from the law, should they return to Arco Iris. Entirely on her own, with no instructions from us, she yanked the plants down from the rafters and threw them out the back window of the cabin.

When the cops and I arrived at the cabin, we saw Jenny sitting there on the porch, her little feet dangling, rocking her legs like nothing's going on. The cops pushed past her, rampaged around the cabin a few times, and then circled around back. There lay the six straggly plants.

"Caught you red-handed," said the sheriff, as they prodded Jenny and me back up the road, where they loaded all five of us into the squad cars and hauled us in.

"Do you not have anything more important to do than arresting women, old people, and children?" I always had to say my piece. Shiner sat next to me whispering, "Hush. We're in enough trouble."

Ultimately, they decided to book only me. I got two years' probation for the pot plants, along with a $2,000 fine. When word went out on the invisible feminist wire that SunHawk had been targeted, a woman up North put up the money for me. I thanked her and went about my business.

*/ */ */

*These men in boots on a search-and-destroy mission through our garden could
not comprehend the bounty of our Mother Earth. Here on our mountain, we
have cultivated herbals, medicinals, flowers, and food to sustain body and soul.
We pray to Tonantzin, Our Mother, with gratitude for the blessings She gives
us, year after year, in Her endless generosity: rosemary, basil, sage, rue, oregano,
wormwood, thyme, Russian comfrey, spearmint, peppermint, elderberry, shiitake
mushrooms, stevia, lemon balm, oxeye daisies, passionflower, chicory, potatoes,
onions, garlic, parsley, cilantro, Swiss chard, spinach, arugula, mustard, cucum-
bers, tomatoes, peppers (cayenne, jalapeño, Anaheim, Thai chili), corn, squash
(heirloom, summer, zucchini, pumpkin), beans, wine berries, loofahs, gourds . . .
Tlatzokamati.*

🌿 🌿 🌿

Life on the mountain continued. We did not let the fugitive women's desperate acts or the locals' mean spirits cloud our vision for Arco Iris. Women
and children kept finding their way to us. Some stayed for days, some for
weeks or months or years.

One woman would remain on the land for almost three decades: Luisa
Cruz, child of the projects, child of Queens, New York, a tirelessly hard
worker, with razor-sharp intelligence and radical womanist politics and
some hard-edged humor, with a stone-cold butch shield and swagger, and
a fire behind her eyes ready to ignite.

She arrived ready to put her carpentry skills to work. I barely noticed
her. I had my hands full feeding kids, caring for an elder, building a dwelling
from the ground up. I was not looking for anything.

Shiner had taken Frannie and the kids into town to do laundry and buy
groceries. That excursion took a few days. Alone on the land, Luisa and I
worked with our shirts off in the midsummer heat. Holding my hammer
high, I glanced over at her on the roof of the framed-out house structure.
Lean and muscular, with firm breasts that jumped with each swing of her
hammer, she worked with precision. My hammer-wielding arm went weak.
My womb seized inward. When she looked up and caught me looking at
her, I managed to keep my gaze steady. In that instant, we both knew.

After the day's work, she slipped off to the cabin. Months later, she
confessed that she washed up especially well that evening, the whole time
telling herself, "Now, I don't need to be doing anything. I do not!" I too

cleaned up before walking down to the cabin, where she met me with her skin still damp, and her voice thick and soft all at once.

"May I come in?" I asked.

We spent the night talking. But we both knew.

In the morning, I went down the road to call Shiner, who was still in town with the kids and Frannie. "I just want to let you know. This is what I'm going to do. Luisa is the person I've been waiting for. I didn't know it until yesterday. Now I know."

✿ ✿ ✿

At Christmastime, we traveled to Dallas for our huge extended-family celebration. Hundreds of people gathered in a vast hall. Laughter lifted through the air. Spanish words danced from our tongues. Tables buckled under domes and platters of special home-cooked Mexican holiday foods.

Mom found me quickly in the crowd. She pulled me aside and looked solemnly into my eyes as she removed the treasured turquoise ring, simple but artistically crafted, from her finger. She placed it in the palm of my hand, pressing my fingers around it as she closed her eyes in prayer. "It is late, and Suzanna has not arrived," she said. "She is in trouble. Go get her, now."

I first found a phone to call Suzanna. She cried, "Help me, please! There are snakes, snakes everywhere in my apartment! I tried to leave but they were in the car!"

Suzanna had spoken before of the jealous ex-girlfriend of an Indian man she had started seeing: Esmeralda, whose family practiced witchcraft. I knew I faced a spiritual battle, my first with black magic.

I rushed into the apartment with my sage burning, the smoke opening a safe path. I smudged, prayed, chanted loudly. Suzanna cowered in a corner. "They are everywhere," she sobbed. "Snakes, everywhere!"

Though I could not see the snakes, I felt their presence. I felt a black energy thick in the room as I rushed to my sister, grabbing her arm and dragging her toward the door, which I had intentionally left open. My mother's protection radiated through the ring, slashing the darkness, flinging us through the doorway into sun-filtered dusk.

Mom showed little outward expression when we arrived back at the gathering. She embraced Suzanna and shot me a look of deep gratitude.

✐ ✐ ✐

La familia had an off-and-on presence on the land. Many came repeatedly. Suzanna and Lalo each visited us a few times in the early years. Diane came more regularly, and Jesús, while catapulting into international fame as a sculptor, made his way up our rough road on numerous occasions. Nieces and nephews, both mine and Luisa's, often spent whole summers with us. Aunties, cousins, and more far-flung blood relations visited too.

My sister Diane considered moving to the land at one point, with her two children. Her son JR, at the age of thirteen, had been shot five times in the stomach while simply walking home one afternoon; he survived, with permanent injuries. Diane was ready to leave Dallas. When we heard that a little café in Ponca had closed down, we saw an opportunity. We would open a Mexican restaurant there, where Diane would cook and we would all work! We let our hopes soar, until we hit another wall of prejudice. None of the locals, and no bank, would help us, despite Diane's good credit and steady income as a federal employee. That disappointment took the wind out of us for a while.

Mom and Dad proved to be the steadiest of all the visitors from la familia. Each year for many years, they made their way up the mountain, bringing supplies they felt we might need. Along with the expensive Honda generator Dad brought when we began construction on the house, he also lugged up the rutted road an old trailer loaded with unclaimed freight insulation and various building materials. One year Mom brought me beautiful deerskin moccasins, which I wore to shreds. The traditional healer's clothes she brought—the white, gathered skirts and embroidered blouses and flowing Mexican dresses—these I treasured as sacred garments. I still keep them with much care.

Though we lived in the wild, we always lived in community and with family, the given and the chosen. *Tlatzokamati.*

11

Love and Loss

On our mountain, we could forget the troubles of the world for weeks at a time. We lived fully off the grid in those early years, often learning of others' joys and calamities after considerable delay.

That is how the devastating news about Princess came to us here on the land, the news that the daughter of our sister Isis had been murdered in a carjacking in DC at the age of nineteen. Weeks passed before we learned that Isis had raced home to bury her child. Months passed before she reappeared on the land, angrier and sadder than ever. The longstanding nickname of Mama Bear, applied to her affectionately to describe her general grumpiness, took on new meaning in the months and years and decades after Princess died.

With Sassafras in disarray as the white women fled, leaving the women of color on the land with no legal standing or financial resources, Isis decided to settle at Arco Iris. She moved into the old one-room cabin, where she slept night and day, crawling out occasionally to eat, smoke, and complain. We let her be.

Even at her best, Isis had never been much of a manual worker. She had been an office worker in DC. She was physically small. When she accompanied me to haul firewood, she would put one piece on the truck for every four of mine. As much as she liked being on the land, being in nature, she was not cut out all that well for the rugged work we needed to do to keep Arco Iris going. Isis liked to cook. She dabbled in jewelry making, some beadwork. She made art. She wrote poetry. Eventually, over the years, as I built lodges and held Ceremony, and as we practiced the ways of the Ancestors, Isis became my go-to fire keeper, a sacred role she never neglected. But back in those times of raw anguish, she did not work and could not work.

Then one day, as winter took hold on the mountain, Isis made an announcement. "I will teach the children," she said. "That's what I can do."

We had four children living on the land at that time: Jenny, Kelly, and a niece and nephew of mine. Within a few days, a pattern emerged. They would trot down to the cabin on those winter mornings, all energy and fire, only to find Isis asleep and the wood-burning stove gone cold. Minutes later, they would return to me. "It's too cold down there," they would say. "Isis hasn't lit the stove and the cabin is freezing. She's hiding under the covers and won't get out." Luisa and I would go down there, start the fire, get the cabin warmed up and the teacher thawed out. Then the kids would come bouncing back down the path, in size order, with Jenny leading the pack.

"Jenny is a little devil," Isis began to say. "A conniving little devil." She grumbled on.

As anyone who ever met her knew, Jenny was the most people-pleasing child imaginable. So were the others. Not a troublemaker among them.

Then Isis came up to the clearing one day, shouting, "I hate them! I hate them all. I hate kids!"

"Isis, you don't mean that," I said.

Luisa stepped in. "Isis says she hates kids? Believe her."

"I can't do it. I'm not doing it. I'm done. I am not going to be a teacher." Isis stomped off toward the cabin.

Shortly thereafter, she moved to Eureka Springs with some of the women of color who had left Sassafras. That didn't work out either.

In 1981, Diana Rivers and nineteen other white women bought land in Madison County, closer to Fayetteville. Ozarks Land Holding Association, they named it. Diana posted the original down payment on the 140 acres. Each member then paid in for a five-acre plot to build and live on, with usage rights to the commonly owned buildings and land. Lesbian-separatist from the start, OLHA never pretended to be open to all comers or communal in structure. New members had to be vetted by the community, and everyone had to pay in to become a member. The carefully drawn-up bylaws specified that all community decisions, including membership matters, would operate on a system of "consensus minus one."

Isis, being Isis, would never pass that admission test. She irked everyone at some point. Besides, she was dirt poor, living off disability, donations, and very occasional paid work.

In time, Diana had a tiny house built for Isis on some land she owned across the creek from OLHA. Some gay guys lived there too. Over the years, she also provided Isis with vehicles. What motivated Diana, I never fully understood. She did care about Isis, loved her, maybe even identified with her in some way, having also lost a child. Call it what you will, it never felt right to me, the layout over there at OLHA, with the relatively prosperous white women on one side of the creek and the only woman of color, along with two gay men, on the other side.

With Luisa on the land and in my life, my awareness of the wider world sharpened. I had begun already to connect with Indigenous people, medicine women and men, healers and shamans across the Americas. I had already planted myself on the side of justice for women, children, and people of color; for those without wealth and inherited advantage; and for our Mother Earth. Luisa helped me dig even deeper into this rich soil. I began to see my own life experiences—as a Latina, as a Two-Spirit woman, as a person born into poverty—in new ways. Sadly, in the course of my awakenings, I felt myself drifting away from Shiner, who took this hard.

Frannie had become clingier. She had lived on the land for about three years already—and that old lady was healthy. While her mind had flown, her tiny body, weighing at most one hundred pounds, held on. She took no medications. And she would accept care from no one but Shiner. When I approached, she flapped her arms and let out deep, panicked noises. (Granted, my appearance might have shocked any urban society lady of the time: I typically wore a headband, no shirt, a breechcloth, and a belt with a sheathed buck knife attached.) With Shiner nearby, Frannie purred. They spent a lot of time together in the RV.

Frannie started to grow an umbilical cord, a literal extension of flesh sprouting from her navel that measured over two inches long. I had a bad feeling about it. "Be careful, Shiner," I warned. "She can suck your energy out. Maintain your space, your psychic space."

✒ ✒ ✒

Coming of Age Ceremony at Rainbow Land

It is spring of 1983, and we gather here on the mountain at Arco Iris to celebrate and honor my daughter Jennifer Jo Moroles as she comes into womanhood. Jennifer will soon be twelve.

On this day, Father Sky's majestic blue expanse and Grandfather Sun's bright rays oversee the rebirth of the land. The morning's white cloud mist rises from the swift creek below our home, as nature's orchestra, running free, carries the gurgle of wet-weather springs and the trills and swishes of birds in song and flight.

It is an auspicious day.

Our Mother Earth, ever-changing woman, has dressed for the sacred occasion. Her trees wear new leaves, every shade of green. Wild spring flowers abound: yellow daffodils, dog's-tooth violets, celandine poppies, white bloodroot, violet phlox, bright-red cardinal lobelia. Miniature blue irises blanket the leaf-covered ground. Wild, sweet-smelling pink azaleas share their scent.

The women of Arco Iris welcome our rainbow sisters as they arrive. My birth sister Diane and her children come from Dallas with a handcrafted Ceremonial dress for Jennifer's special day. Jennifer's godmother, Marsha Gómez, and her partner, Clary Pérez, swoop in from Austin. Other women of color from the Sassafras women's commune on the twin mountain across the creek, Jenny's wild adopted aunties, make a joyous appearance.

All arrive bearing handmade gifts and food for our feast after the Temescal Ceremony.

Oh happy day for the women of Arco Iris: my partner Shiner and her grandmother, Frances; my partner Luisa; our young, adopted daughter, Kelly; and Jennifer Jo, radiant in the long, white Ceremonial dress, her hair braided, her pleasure both modest and unabashed.

When the lodge fire is ready, we bow low to enter the Ceremony lodge in a show of humility. As I was taught, I lead our Ceremony in four rounds of prayer.

We begin with the East. The red lava rocks, our awakened Ancestors, are brought in.

We give our deepest appreciation and thanks for the privilege to enter into our Mother's Earth womb.

We honor Her and all the Spirits with sweet cedar greens, incense placed on the glowing lava.

We ask for guidance and blessings.

We honor the Spirits of the Land and all our relations of the East, and the winged Eagle who helps us see from our highest selves.

Each woman offers prayers for the beginning of Jennifer's womanhood and honoring the end of her childhood.

And so for the South, the West, and the North.

We also bow as we leave the lodge, in a show of gratitude for all we have received.

As each comes out of the lodge, she rinses off with cold water pumped from our cistern and dresses in clean, nice Ceremony clothes, representing newness and rebirth.

Jenny humbly receives the handmade gifts from her family and community. Then we feast and celebrate around a fire, with stories and laughter.

After a long day, we are thankful as we go off to our beds. I beam with pride for my child, Jennifer, born now into womanhood.

Tlatzokamati.

Luisa, Jenny, and I went to a Latina women's conference in Malibu with some of the women from Sassafras. We left Shiner, Frannie, and Kelly on the land. Several of us tan-skinned and brown-skinned land women, with the smell of hardwood smoke soaked into our hair and clothing, piled into an old pickup for the road trip. Apparently, we stood out from the city women gathered at the conference—enough for the local newspaper to run a piece on us.

Toward the end of the meeting, Shiner somehow managed to get a call through to me. Sobbing, she told me that Frannie had died on the land, in her sleep. "It's all done, SunHawk. I executed the plan."

We had prepared carefully for this moment, never imagining that Shiner would face it alone. We had discussed it down to the details. If Frannie died on the land, we did not want to risk having the coroner come out, with the sheriff trailing along. While we had absolutely nothing to hide, we'd been burnt enough by these boys who itched for another "caught you red-handed" look at what the lesbian, Indian, outlaw witches might be doing.

When Frannie breathed her last, we had decided, we would lay her body on a mattress in the bed of our land truck. We would then place another mattress over her, tie the bundle up to avoid the body getting beaten up on the rough road down the mountain, and head into Fayetteville to a friend's house, as we often did to wash our laundry and cook. From there, with Frannie transferred to a bed, we would call the coroner to report that Grandmother had died.

Shiner managed all of that alone, while comforting Kelly and alerting her own parents in San Francisco to the death. The Cardozos told her to have the body cremated in Fayetteville and then come straight away to Minneapolis, can of ashes in hand, for a small family service.

"My father will pay to fly you up there," Shiner told me. "I need you there."

We hightailed it back to Arkansas in the rusted-out pickup. In Fayetteville, I boarded a plane for Minnesota, where the family shed tears for Frannie, when they were not fixated on my "Indian garb," as they called it.

Shiner spiraled down far and fast in the weeks and months after Frannie died. Grief took her voice. It squelched her appetite. It stole her smile. She would wander into the woods for hours, in the depths of winter. We could not stop her. Each day as darkness approached, I took the dogs with me to find her and bring her home. Sometimes she resisted.

Jenny had turned twelve that past summer, celebrated by la familia and friends in a lodge Ceremony on the land. In her quiet way, she entered her womanhood. Now she observed us, her adults, frozen in place.

One day, Jenny ushered Luisa and me into the tipi. We tried not to smile as the solemn little adult addressed us. "Shiner is not okay, and she needs to go. She needs to go home with her parents. Mom, you need to tell her that."

I did as told. "I'm worried about you, Shiner," I said. "Go home and be with your family for a while. When you start feeling better, you can come back."

The whole drive to Dallas, Shiner cried. I cried. Neither of us wanted her to leave; both of us knew it had to be. We clung to each other for a long time at the airport, beyond words. I plunged my face into her curls one last time before she caught her flight to San Francisco and a new phase of life.

∕ ∕ ∕

Luisa and I took our little family to the beach in Tampico, Mexico, to get our heads and hearts together after that. In our battered little truck, we stopped first in Dallas and then in Rockport to visit family. Mom fussed over Kelly and Jenny, buying them Easter dresses and hats and baskets. Then Dad drove us to the border in Reynosa, Mexico, where we caught a bus to Tampico.

We set out with just enough money to pay for transport, food, and the cheapest of lodgings for a week. Over the border, our bus had to detour inland to skirt a hurricane. The extra day ate away at our food budget.

A small, somewhat hunched woman befriended us on the bus. She wore a shroud of sadness. I sensed it strongly beneath the tenderness she showed our girls. She touched their hair; she fed them from her own stash of tortillas. As the bus approached a muddy village back on route to Tampico, she said, "I'll be getting off here. Come, stay with me for a couple of days until the storm passes." With a silent glance, Luisa and I decided to accept her offer.

Though I don't remember her name or the name of the town, I will forever remember that we slept that night, Luisa and I, in a small bedroom, spare of furniture and bare-walled except for one framed photograph, eight by ten, of a young boy with a stern, hard-jawed expression on his face.

"What is it?" I asked Luisa. "He doesn't look right."

Around midnight, the dogs in the tiny village began to bark. They barked and barked. A wind blew through our open window, spreading the sheer white curtains wide.

Luisa bolted up in bed. "Look, look at that picture. It's glowing!"

I calmed her, rocked her, held her until her breath signaled sleep. I, too, saw a golden light illuminating the photo of the little boy.

I sat up, closed my eyes, and meditated on what this could be about. After a few minutes, I sensed a presence in the room.

"*Quién es?*" I asked. "Who is it?"

"Por favor, señora, tell my mother that I am all right. Please, tell her to let me go. All will be fine." He had the piping voice of a school-aged boy.

In the morning, I asked the woman about the photograph.

"He was our only child," she said. "He was eight years old when he died in the bathtub. I had gone into the kitchen to prepare dinner for my husband."

"Did he drown?"

"No. He simply died. My husband never forgave me. He left too."

I knew that I had to perform Ceremony. She agreed to a tarot reading. The cards revealed that the child lingered in an in-between place.

"There is a time for everything," I said. "This is the time to let him go. Release him to heaven. He asks this of you."

She fingered her rosary and nodded.

We left shortly after that. Luisa would not spend another night in that room.

ABOVE LEFT
María Cristina's mother, María
Bautista Moroles, pictured
picking cotton in South Texas
as a migrant worker, age fifteen.
Author photo

ABOVE RIGHT
Baby María Cristina with her
mother, 1953, Corpus Christi,
Texas. *Author photo*

LEFT
María Bautista posing in the Dallas
housing projects with the four
eldest Moroles siblings (from left
to right): Joe Jr., Jesús, Diana,
and María Cristina. *Author photo*

ABOVE LEFT
María Cristina at age eighteen with baby Jenny, 1971, Dallas, Texas. *Author photo*

ABOVE RIGHT
Vicky Cryer in the Arizona desert, 1976. *Author photo*

LEFT
Jenny with her grandmother María Bautista in front of the Moroles family home in West Dallas, Texas, 1972. *Author photo*

OPPOSITE
María Cristina, now identifying as SunHawk, in front of her first self-made tipi home, 1977. *Author photo*

Jenny, Leona Garcia, SunHawk, and Shiner (Patti Cardozo) pictured with their first land truck and packing a pony before heading up the road to Arco Iris. *Author photo*

Sheila "Isis" Brown at Sassafras, around 1977. *Author photo*

ABOVE
From the left: Marsha Gómez, Burning Cloud, and Isis, part of the Sassafras Women of Color Collective. *Author photo*

MIDDLE
Chief Louis Farmer, chief of the Onondaga Six Nations of the Iroquois Confederacy, with SunHawk. *Author photo*

BELOW
From the left: the Moroles sisters—Suzanna, Diana, and SunHawk—in SunHawk's house at Arco Iris during construction. *Author photo*

ABOVE
Nightdancer, SunHawk's beloved horse. *Author photo*

MIDDLE LEFT
Shiner and Jenny Jo Moroles. *Author photo*

BELOW
Jenny in front of the tipi before her Coming of Age Ceremony, Arco Iris, 1983. *Author photo*

OPPOSITE ABOVE
Jenny with her godmother, Marsha Gómez, in the outside kitchen at Arco Iris after Jenny's Coming of Age Ceremony. *Author photo*

OPPOSITE MIDDLE
Diné grandmother Effie Yazzie, on a visit to Arco Iris from the rez in 1986, teaching SunHawk how to finish her Navajo rug on a homemade cedar loom. *Author photo*

OPPOSITE BELOW
Baby Mario in the cradleboard made by SunHawk, 1988. *Author photo*

OPPOSITE ABOVE
Baby Mario with his auntie Burning Cloud. *Author photo*

OPPOSITE LEFT
SunHawk's parents, José Elizondo and María Bautista, in front of their Rockport, Texas, home after going fishing. *Author photo*

OPPOSITE BELOW
SunHawk and her big brother Jesús behind a granite sculpture in his Rockport, Texas, studio. *Author photo*

ABOVE
Bolivian *chamán* Froilan Monzon Zegarra with SunHawk, after training initiation in the Mesa Ceremony in Lima, Peru. *Author photo*

RIGHT
Doña Julieta, *curandera* Oaxaqueña, who specialized in magic-mushroom medicine, with SunHawk, after exchanging gifts, 1993. *Author photo*

OPPOSITE
SunHawk and Jenny in front of new road signs for Camino Arco Iris and La Clínica. *Author photo*

ABOVE
Cynthia Pérez, Mililani Trask, and SunHawk at the Two-Spirit Women Activists Gathering. *Author photo*

RIGHT
Mario after his two-day Coming of Age Ceremony, known as a Vision Quest, 2000. *Author photo*

ABOVE
SunHawk and Señora Cobb, the West
Coast leader of the Danza Azteca,
exchanging gifts in Sacramento,
California. *Author photo*

LEFT
SunHawk, now known as Águila,
with her "big sister" Juanita Arriaga
Frost during the annual Caminata
Ceremony. *Author photo*

OPPOSITE
Águila with Lucia López Hall,
staunch advocate of Arco Iris and
Arco Iris Earth Care Project Board
of Directors member for over two
decades. *Author photo*

OPPOSITE ABOVE
Jenny with her partner, Lisa Miller, on the land. *Author photo*

OPPOSITE BELOW
Águila with her teacher Ranjana Pallana, 2022. *Author photo*

RIGHT
Águila with her niece Victoria Moroles and dogs Django and Junko, Arco Iris, 2022. *Author photo*

BELOW
Águila's off-grid, double-envelope, passive-solar home, built completely by Two-Spirit women's hands. *Author photo*

Águila spending time
with Grandmother Cedar,
Santuario Arco Iris, 2023.
Author photo

Grandmother Cedar,
growing from a boulder,
2023. *Author photo*

12

Tonantzin, Mother Earth

I knew by then that I had been entrusted with sacred healing powers. About their full extent, I still had much to learn. Again and again, I sought out teachers who could inch me a step further along my path. Several times, I found my way to medicine women in Mexico and across the US. Each took me into her home, allowing me to observe her practice. From time to time, I met with the Diné, Mena, and Hopi medicine women. From a *curandera* in Oaxaca, I learned Temescal Ceremony; from another, I learned Hongo Ceremony. Eventually I learned Ayahuasca Ceremony from abuela María Alice Campos Freire, of the International Council of Thirteen Indigenous Grandmothers, whom I had met at the Cheyenne reservation and later visited in Portland.

My friends Leon Shenandoah—Tadadaho, or chief of chiefs, of the Six Nations of the Iroquois Confederacy—and Louis Farmer, chief of the Onondaga, counseled with me when I met troubles along the way. I got to know them well. Sometimes I was called upon to drive these and other chiefs to gatherings, traveling long distances with the most esteemed elders in my care. All of them helped me on my journey for many years, some for decades.

Chief Louis Farmer came to Arco Iris in 1983. He stayed for over a week with us, after an Onondaga elder, a seer, told him to return here with me from New York, where I had gone to seek his counsel about the land. "You need to go there and do Ceremony," she told him. On the land, he rested and reflected before leading a Ceremony of the Dead to awaken the Ancestors of this land to aid and protect us. Once awakened, the Ancestors helped us to develop La Caminata, our most sacred Ceremony here on Rainbow Land. Each spring, we call the Ancestors to bless the land as we walk its periphery, in all four directions, in prayer and pilgrimage. Chief Louis Farmer gave us that gift.

Of all the medicine men I met, Phillip Deere lived deepest in my heart. I had met him when I was twenty years old and hungry for spiritual guidance. I had followed Swami Muktananda to Oklahoma to commune with the Native American medicine women and men, elders, and chiefs. It hit me with a bang that day: They looked alike, these brown and tan people, from India or Oklahoma or New York or Canada or Mexico, all healers sharing sacred traditions, seeking truth, honoring the Ancestors and teaching the children to live gently on our Earth. I needed to go home, I realized in that moment, not to my parents' house, but to my people. Phillip Deere ushered me home. Over the years, he initiated me into the Muscogee Creek medicine ways. He taught me Ceremony. He entrusted me with lodge keeping. He gave me responsibilities that were handed only to people who had earned them. He accepted us as Two Spirits when many in the community did not.

In 1985, as the time of year for his annual Indigenous Elders and Youth Conference approached, I called him.

"My body is sick," he told me. "I am not well." I asked if we could come early. I offered to do some healing work with him, herbs and touch and energy, from the teachers and traditions I had been studying for many years by then. "Yes, come," he said. "I need strong medicine."

Just short of Phillip's place in Oklahoma, our old truck sputtered out on I-40. Luisa, Jenny, Kelly, and I collected our gear, abandoned the vehicle, and arrived on foot at the meeting grounds.

Everything seemed different that year. Normally exuberant people seemed somber. Phillip's eldest daughter, a Christian who had not grown up in the Ceremony way, had taken the mantle of leadership from her father, who was much sicker than he had let on. And for the first time in my awareness, a white person had not only underwritten the gathering, offering untold resources from her inherited oil fortune, but she also attended our sacred Ceremony.

I went to see Phillip. A guard stood at his door—a young, fierce-looking Indian warrior who would not let me in without Phillip's express permission. "She may come in," I heard my old friend say.

He lay with his head propped on pillows, his graying hair braided, one eye pushed forward by a tumor behind the socket. His time left on this Earth could not be long. I felt that to be true, although I could not fully take it in.

I needed to work on every level. I smudged him and his small home, and then I prepared a poultice and made him some tea. We spoke only briefly; he was weak. I asked if I could come each day to treat him. "I would like that," he said. A brief smile creased his good eye; his gold tooth glinted.

When I went the next day, again dressed in my white traditional healer's clothes with a red sash, two giant warriors flanked the doorway. They met me this time with more assertiveness. "Who are you? What's your business here? Who said you can come in?"

"Phillip," I said, and they let me pass.

I had smudged the room and placed a poultice on his eye, as I had done the day before, when a woman bolted into the room, firing questions at me. "What are you doing here? What do you want? Why are you trying to see my father? You're not a medicine woman. You're not doing anything to my father."

I switched calmly into warrior mode, knowing my responsibility to protect both Phillip and myself in that moment. "I never said I was a medicine woman. Phillip Deere has been my teacher for many years, and he is my friend. I have been a healer for many years now. I asked Phillip's permission to come, and he granted that."

"Well, you don't have my permission!" Her breath whistled through her teeth. I could see her counting my deficits: I was not of their tribe. I was young. I was a Two Spirit. I would not bend to her authority. "I don't trust you," she said at last. "I'm the eldest daughter. The only way you can treat my father is if you can get the permission from all the elders."

I knew the elders, all of them. Each year, I gathered with them. They saw that Phillip trusted me. Some, I knew, harbored homophobic attitudes. Yet even they knew I was not going to do anything harmful to Phillip. I went to speak to each of these leaders individually and asked to counsel with them that very day. Every single one—Leon Shenandoah, Louis Farmer, Janet

McCloud, Thomas Banyacya, Dan Evehema, George Kingfisher—gave me their blessing to return each day to treat Phillip with the strongest medicine I had. They said prayers to bless me in that endeavor.

When I went back to the first daughter to tell the elders' decision, she lost her resolve. For about a minute. I took that pause to go to Phillip's bedside with my medicine bag filled with herbs and offerings from Arco Iris.

The following day, when I came back with my medicine, the eldest met me with the warriors. She seemed on a crusade. "You may not go in," she said. "And you and your people are to leave the land immediately. Now!"

I first went to the roundhouse to do my prayers around the sacred fire. The warriors waited quietly at a distance. Next, I summoned my power to tell *mi familia*. I found Jenny and Kelly in the kitchen with the women, and Luisa doing the men's work of preparing for a lodge. "We have to go," I said. "We will go in peace." We gathered our gear.

Everyone at the gathering knew us from years past. We had many friends. News traveled quickly: We had been kicked out, sent away, banished from Phillip Deere's land in Muskogee and from the national gathering.

A hush came over the people as we began to walk down the long, flat dirt road toward the gate. Some single file, some in groups of two or three—our many supporters trailed silently behind us, shoes kicking up dust along the path of this, our long walk.

Suddenly one of Phillip's little granddaughters, maybe eight years old, came running up to me. She grabbed my leg. "Don't go. Jenny! Kelly!" she called out to her friends.

I stopped and talked to the child, the only one to speak directly to us. "We have to go. We are going to be okay."

She wept. "Don't leave. Please stay."

I knelt to look her in the eyes. "I love you, sweet daughter. You're brave. You're wise. You will be a great medicine woman someday. Please tell Phillip for me that we had to leave and that we did not want to. We were asked to leave." I removed one of my earrings and pressed it into her hand. "Remember us and remember this day."

We walked with our heads high. We did not look back. We walked right through the entrance gate and on toward the highway, where I stuck my thumb out for a ride.

Within seconds, the oil heiress from the gathering, a woman probably in her forties, pulled up alongside us in her van. She had heard what was going on and raced out to find us. She was the only white person there, as far as I could tell. A philanthropist of good causes, she must have found our expulsion troubling. "Hop in," she called out her window. "I'll take you out to the bus station, and I'll give you some bus fare." On the way, she deluged us with questions: "Who are you? Where do you live? What do you do there? What can I do to help you?" We could barely speak, in our sorrow.

Ella Alford was her name. Over the next few years, she became one of our funders, when we found ourselves strapped. She came several times out to the mountain. Later her daughter came to the land.

Phillip died soon after the gathering. Here on the land, without a telephone, we did not hear of his passing in time to pay our respects in person to this great mentor, teacher, and friend.

Not long after that, one of the elders from the gathering, George Kingfisher, brought a group of young warriors to Arco Iris to help us dig a cellar. They stayed for a week, digging the hole and drinking in the beauty of our Rainbow Land in the Ozarks. We remained in the fold. *Tlatzokamati.*

Luisa and I had been doing work for battered women through a shelter in Harrison. The director there was married to a progressive lawyer in town who helped us out occasionally with legal matters concerning the land. We visited him one day in 1986 to discuss the process of incorporating as a nonprofit.

After warm greetings all the way around, he said, "I'm going to have to ask you something. It has come to my attention through my wife that the sheriff's department is looking for a little girl who was kidnapped by her foster mother. Her name is Kelly."

A knife in the heart could not have hurt me more. Kelly had been with us for more than three years. Her mother, Robyn, had our information. She could have written to us. In fact, Robyn's sister had reached out to us, so they knew how to find us in a peaceful way. Robyn and I had an agreement, mother to mother. I always told Kelly her mom would come back for her someday, when she had gotten herself ready.

"Yes, that's us," I told the lawyer.

"I was afraid it was y'all. I didn't say anything to them, but now I'm legally bound to let them know." He told us how to proceed. "We're going to try to get this all ironed out so you don't get in trouble." He did that for us.

We contacted Human Services and made a plan for them to come out for a preliminary home visit. They informed me that Robyn had flown in from Minneapolis. She would join them on this initial visit, to reconnect with her daughter and begin a gradual process of reunification.

For two days, we prepared. We spiffed up the house, which we kept neat and clean anyway. Kelly gathered her favorite books, to show off her reading skills to her mother; I had been teaching her. She laid her favorite toys out on her bed, alongside her medicine bag and medicine necklace and the special rocks and feathers she had gathered from the land.

"I'm so excited!" she kept saying. "I'm so scared."

"There's no reason to be scared. She's your mom. She loves you and she misses you. You'll visit here, at home. We'll be with you. Someday, when you're ready, you might go visit her and see Lila."

Because our road was bad and it is so hard for people to find us, we arranged to meet them down at the church and lead them up to the land. Luisa stayed behind preparing lunch while Jenny and I brought Kelly down in the truck.

Two women emerged from the black sedan that idled by the church, one a middle-aged white woman, the other a more together version of Robyn, who had looked strung out when we last saw her.

We pulled up and got out of the truck. Kelly hung back shyly with Jenny as I advanced to greet the women. "You can follow us up the road," I said. "We're three miles up."

The caseworker spoke. "No, we're not going up there. We're leaving from here."

"Leaving?"

"That's right. Don't argue."

"But she doesn't have her things, her toys and her clothes, her precious items."

"She doesn't need any of that."

I turned to Robyn. "Why are you doing this?"

She could hardly look at me. "This is the only way I could afford to get her back."

They gave us two minutes to say our goodbyes before they literally ripped her away, crying and flailing. They stuffed her into the car with the windows up and doors locked and drove off with Kelly screaming at the back window like you see in the movies. She was seven years old when they took her.

In 1994, Jenny and I attended an Indigenous Women's Network conference, with Indigenous women from all over North America, at the White Earth Reservation in northern Minnesota. My friend Winona LaDuke, who was organizing the event, did some legwork to get Robyn's contact information in Minneapolis for me.

Robyn hedged for a couple of days before allowing us ten minutes at her apartment with her daughter, who had grown tall and lithe and beautiful in those eight years, but who also could not meet our eyes. To me Kelly said nothing at all, and to Jenny, only a few words.

I choose to remember the Kelly I knew, loping across the land in moccasins and headband to show each new child who passed through Arco Iris the way to the mountain spring.

We went even further off the grid to help the Diné (Navajo) women at Big Mountain in Arizona who were fighting to stay on their homelands, resisting relocation by the United States government. We stayed about six months in all to support the Indigenous community.

Jenny went to school in Tuba City, where a medicine woman of high repute—the daughter of the Diné elders who were hosting Luisa and me further out on the reservation—served as her host mother for those months. No one messed with her in school, given the honored role of her host in the community, and Jenny thrived in the company of the Indigenous children there.

Out on the rez, we stayed with two elder Diné women, Effie and Louise Yazzie; sometimes their mother, Sosie, stayed with us too. They spoke their traditional language, wore their customary long, gathered, brightly colored skirts, and herded sheep on the hills where uranium dust from mining settled outside and inside every structure and every living being. They had no electricity, only kerosene lights and Coleman lanterns. They spread tablecloths on dirt floors where they ate their mutton and fried bread and swallowed their scalding black coffee. They hauled water, with their grandchildren's help, in fifty-five-gallon drums filled at a well and collected coal by hand from the scraps of the Peabody Mine, which was owned by white people, as was the trading post on the reservation. Each trip to the mine took two days, on unpaved dirt roads. Some Diné women grew beans and squash for sustenance. Most supplemented their diets with government commodities. For other needs, they traded their sheep and their beautiful patterned rugs, handwoven and hand-dyed from the wool of the uranium-dusted sheep.

We became friends with Effie and Louise, communicating mostly through sign language or by drawing pictures. They had no reaction whatsoever to Luisa and me as partners. They drew us into their matriarchal clan, even if we exasperated them by leaving a few sheep behind at the end of our shifts. They would go stomping out through the desert, these old ladies in long skirts, with their dogs and their rifles, to round up the stragglers.

Luisa and I amused them to no end with our headstrong, and sometimes ignorant, ways. The day I hit the gas through a rutted-out stretch of road on the way back from the coal mine, with Effie and Louise in the backseat begging me to slow down as I fishtailed wildly through a huge mud puddle that had mired their truck in muck for hours on the way to the mine—that is the day they decided to adopt us into their clan. I brought the medicine of defiance and practical ingenuity. They began to take me seriously.

They could not understand my disdain for guns, and I had no words to explain the heartbreak that had caused me to shun firearms after my brother Joe's murder. Through example, the Diné elders showed me that a woman with a rifle could protect her sheep from coyotes and settle disputes among men who do not know better than to argue amongst friends. I carried their wisdom back to Arco Iris. They knew more than I did about survival.

I barely survived my time out there. The uranium dust made me sick with jaundice, a relapse from the earlier bouts of hepatitis. The Diné women held a peyote medicine Ceremony for me. I sensed my own people gathered on that dusty land: My mother and tías, my sainted abuelas Antonia and Amá Angelita—all surrounded me in sacred circle as the Diné elders led me through the purges of the night to renewed health by dawn.

Later the government took over Big Mountain, calling it a "national sacrifice area." One by one, the US officials picked off the Diné, in a covert military operation designed to elude national media attention, forcibly relocating them one family at a time to hastily constructed row houses. Many died there, unable to adjust to this unnatural way of life.

13

New Life

Past the spring of my life, in early summer of 1986, I sensed an inner calling, a knowing that I had to do a Vision Quest. I had to immerse myself in Mother Nature and connect with the Universe. I had to seek guidance, understanding, and direction.

For many months I prepared my prayer tobacco ties—small pieces of red cloth with tobacco offerings in each piece, one for each day of the year, each holding a prayer. I strung these pieces together with red yarn to create a sacred-space boundary within which I would stay for the duration of the three days. With my prayer ties as offerings to the Mother and the Universe, to all the creatures—two-legged, four-legged, winged, and finned—I would beseech the Mother to bring the medicine I needed, to summon the medicine of the four sacred directions and the four winds.

In preparation for this Vision Quest, Luisa, Jenny, and I did the Temezcal Ceremony, as a purification for me and to say prayers for my success and protection. They walked me out to the Vision Quest spot, about a mile back into the wilderness on the third bluff away from our home. I wore only my breechcloth and the moccasins my mother had given me and carried only the things that would shield, comfort, and sustain me: a buffalo robe to sit on or wrap myself in, the sacred female medicine pipe, my quart of water to ration, and my medicine bag holding tobacco, cedar, sage, and copal. After setting up my ties in a circle and sanctifying the space with sacred smoke, I watched Luisa, Jenny, and my black lab, Oscura, turn and walk away toward our home. Luisa and Jenny had to coax Oscura, who was reluctant to leave me alone there on the bluff.

For three days and three nights, I prayed for a vision while sipping little bits of water, eating no food, and periodically standing and facing each direction. I prayed to the east for new beginnings and illumination, that the Eagle would teach me to fly high and see from its sharp eye. To the south, as the Serpent of Light wrapped its coils around me, for healing through trust, joy, and innocence. To the west—where the Jaguar pads powerfully, creating and protecting sacred space for death and transformation—as I called in my Ancestors and anyone who would support me in this Spirit journey. And to the north—where the Hummingbird gathers the nectar, the sweetness of life's steadfastness and beauty—to the White-Haired One who carries the sacred bundle of wisdom, knowledge, and universal laws. I begged that She would lay that bundle down with my heart, allow me to share the burden, and that She would open her bundle to let me gather the knowledge and wisdom to remember the sacred laws.

I faced each direction every day, never leaving the sacred ground encompassing perhaps twelve feet in diameter. I begged and cried. I asked the stars at night and Grandmother Moon to illuminate me in the darkness. I prayed and prayed until I felt my thin and frail body disappear. I became earth. I became stone. I became air. I felt no fear. One day, one night, one day, one night—and on the third day, the last day, as the sun began to reach the horizon, I sat there as the Earth herself, the air itself, drifting into the oneness of that sacred space.

As I sat there facing south, I felt a presence in the northeast—the directions of wisdom, knowledge, illumination, and new beginnings coming toward me. I turned to see a big black bear slowly, quietly approaching my circle, her thickly padded paws and huge claws bearing into the earth. She jutted her nose into the air, searching, until she stopped at my sacred boundary of prayer ties, looking straight at me, only six feet away, sensing a presence she somehow could not see.

The wind blew from the southeast, carrying the scent of the bear to Oscura, who had made her way to the bluff, settling herself silently into the forest floor. I did not feel her presence until she charged out of the woods, barking and gnarling at the bear, who gazed calmly at her and then retreated. Unbothered, unafraid, she padded away proudly into the trees.

Bear medicine brings the power of introspection, as the Bear seeks honey, the true nectar or sweetness of life. The Bear emerged from the northwest, indicating the gathering of wisdom, knowledge, and understanding of Universal laws. She continued her journey traveling east, illuminating me to accomplish my goals and dreams.

I knew what we needed to do after the hibernation period of my Vision Quest: We had to bring in new life. We had to call down from the Spirit world, from the heavens, a new life to share this land with us. The sacred little being would be with us soon.

Soon after my Vision Quest, the Spirits tapped me to help bring forth new life. Amira, one of the traveling women who had passed through Arco Iris, moved to Fayetteville with her partner. They wanted to have a baby. Could I help her with the insemination? I said yes.

I went to the Fayetteville address, near the co-op, to see the young Native American man who had agreed to donate sperm. We had set a date for me to collect the medicine. I arrived decked out in the medicine woman way, with my hair all braided and my customary buck knife tucked into the beaded waistband of a long, white cotton skirt.

A different young man answered the door and invited me in. "My roommate left," he said, when I explained my mission.

I looked him over: dark-haired, tan, handsome. I liked his energy. He would do nicely.

"What's your lineage?" I asked.

"Irish and Blackfoot."

"That's good enough. You're going to take your friend's place, because you are here, and it is happening now."

"Now?"

"Yes, now. I'm here to capture the medicine we need to bring a child into life." In full warrior mode, I placed the sterile baby-food jar in his hand and pointed him toward the bathroom. "You're going to do it. You're going to do it because my friend is ready and waiting for me. She has prepared for months for this moment when her moon cycle and the stars are in perfect alignment. I just drove two hours to get here. I need this medicine right now."

He smiled and retreated into the bathroom.

I called out, "Before you do it, I want you to say a prayer. Pray for a happy, healthy baby. That's all we need from you. Just give seed and we will leave you alone."

Back at Amira's place, I held up the tiny jar of medicine. "Are you ready?"

"Yes, I've been praying. I have my altar set up." She and her partner had draped silks and satins around the room. Candles encircled the bed.

"I've done my part. Now you two do your part." I had already instructed them on how to use the turkey baster.

Throughout the Ceremony, I prayed for the little Spirit to come.

The stars had aligned! A pregnancy test confirmed it a month after. Nine months later, little Athena arrived.

✐ ✐ ✐

Luisa and I decided to have a baby. We decided, actually, to have two. They could grow up together. She would go first, as a woman over thirty who had never been pregnant. My fertility had already been tried and found true.

We wanted the babies to have blood from each of our families. For Luisa's donor, we had many choices among the men of my family. I approached the eldest of my male maternal-side cousins—a straightlaced, middle-class engineer. He was also a gifted musician, and single, handsome, and healthy. He made a solid choice for the job, which he agreed to in a heartbeat. Luisa and I would be the parents. He owed nothing beyond the sperm, though he, like every member of la familia, would always be welcome in our lives. We worked it out verbally, never legally. He arranged to drop everything when Luisa's moon cycle aligned with the stars. He had been to the land before, and he loved me. Simple as that.

Mi primo flew from Corpus Christi to Little Rock, rented a car, drove three hours into the mountains, and made his way up our three-mile road after sunset. We had a tipi set up by the pond, with a fire going and the lodge ready. He stripped down to his boxers to join us inside for Ceremony. We prayed for the little Spirit to come to us, the very Spirit who needed us as parents. We called on the little Spirit who could feel the magic in the air that night, as the tipi glowed like a lantern and the owls—eagles of the night, keepers of wisdom—spoke.

He next went up to his cabin with our empty baby-food jar to produce the precious medicine. Tucking the jar into his shirt for the warmth of his breast, he then delivered the donation to us in the tipi and bid us good night.

Luisa and I sat in prayer, the love between us as potent as the night and the stars. Six owls hooted their night song—the song of the Spirit guardians from East, South, West, and North, from Father Sky and from Mother Earth, heralding the arrival of the little Spirit who had journeyed safely to bind our families forever. Everything glowed.

♪ ♪ ♪

We engaged a country midwife, a white mountain woman with a word-of-mouth reputation for safe home deliveries. She made her way out to us several times, never saying much. She would check Luisa over, clucking sometimes about "such slim hips," but never trying to steer us toward a hospital birth. Each visit, she pulled me aside to talk about preparing the birthing room—our bedroom—with clean towels and pillows, lots of boiled water, and a collection of herbs: leaves from the wild red raspberry for an easier delivery; blue cohosh to speed it up in the final stages; blackberry leaves and rose petals as astringents in case of hemorrhage; and for the child, sage to cure thrush. I listened carefully to her advice and added to my store of herbs and tinctures throughout the pregnancy.

In November, with the February due date fast approaching, the midwife came to examine Luisa. Then she took me aside. "This will be my last visit," she said. "My husband will not allow it."

I felt the blood bolt through my body, sharp as ice. "Please don't say this. You see how far back on the land we are. Why would you do this to us?"

"You are pagans." She looked down. "He won't allow it." She gathered her items into her bag and spoke her parting words. "I'm concerned for her because she has a very narrow pelvis and I expect it to be a difficult birth. I'm sorry."

We put out word for a midwife who would take us on in the third trimester, with us living way back here, in the middle of winter, with snow likely to fall soon. None available or willing. Nor could we simply abandon our farm. So we sprang into action. I got all the books on midwifery I could locate and undertook intensive study, hours each day for weeks. Through the mail, I ordered a midwifery kit. We contacted our community—women of color, lesbian women—for hands-on support. Who could come out to the land to help us keep the house warm, carry in wood, haul water, and keep our little farm running smoothly in the uncertain period before and after the birth? Who could also assist Jenny and me with the birth? Our good friend Lola, a Chinese woman, traveled from Chicago with her partner, Laura. A white friend of Luisa's came from Little Rock, and our old friend Burning Cloud, a Filipina and Nisqually woman who lived then in Fayetteville, joined us. With these good sisters on the land awaiting the birth, helping with the chores, and tending to Luisa in the last couple of weeks as her belly expanded out from her slim hips, I felt confident that we could bring the new little being safely into this life.

✗ ✗ ✗

Her water broke at the very beginning of the labor. Twenty-four hours of dry labor later, Luisa lay motionless and silent on our bed, too weak even to moan, let alone resist the urge to push. On examination, I could feel the top of the baby's head beginning to squeeze through, a two-inch segment of skull, like a lemon. Yet her cervix had not dilated enough for safe passage. Luisa's eyes rolled back in her head. I could feel her slipping away from consciousness. We were losing them, mother and child.

In despair, I called all of the women into the bedroom, the birthing room. "We must focus. This room is a womb. We are all energy. We will push this baby out with our energy. Now everyone all at once: Push!" The room contracted; it heaved. "Push!" We all gasped as the tiny head appeared in full, and the shoulders, and then the baby slipped out, squawking and red, decidedly male, and Luisa came to full consciousness, reaching for her baby boy. We placed little Mario on her chest as we cut the cord and collapsed into one another's arms, all of us overjoyed to have brought forth life.

Burning Cloud, who had a bit of irreverence in her, laughed when she saw the lump on the side of Mario's head. "Somebody hit him with a baseball bat?" she asked. "What are we going to do about that lump?"

I pulled out a little cotton knit hat and put it on the baby. "Good enough for now!"

✗ ✗ ✗

Not much later, Luisa began to spike a fever. I took Mario from her so she could sleep. Placing him on my chest, I noticed that he labored for breath. After a spell, I felt Luisa's forehead again. Scorching. And Mario's tiny lungs strained harder at each in-breath. We had done everything we could under the circumstances. Now, I knew, we needed to seek medical attention.

Leaving the others behind to take care of the place, Lola and I loaded Luisa and Mario into the truck, which we inched and slid down our icy road as fast as we dared, our precious ones wrapped in blankets, our hearts locked in the timeless resolve that keeps panic at bay. We had to get them to the closest hospital, in Harrison. My fingers pressed white on the wheel. I drove the winding route down Highway 43 in record time.

The white-haired, white-skinned, white-coated doctor yelled at us from the first word he spoke. "You could have killed her! And this baby!" He started to examine Luisa, wrinkling his face in disgust. "She stinks. She's rotten. Rotting inside. You did that to her." He said exactly that. We, of course, could not see that she had a tear inside, a festering infection.

We had been up for thirty hours. We were exhausted. When the doctor next turned to examine Mario, I would not let him.

"Give me that baby!" he yelled.

"No, you're not touching him."

He shouted some more at me. I would not hand the baby to him. "You can examine him right here, now, while I hold him."

"Then I won't examine him." He left abruptly, muttering under his breath.

I told the nurse, "I want another doctor, a woman doctor."

They called in Dr. Chambers, a woman, who spoke gently to me. "I can check him right there where you are." She did that, and then asked to read our delivery notes.

Mario needed to be helicoptered to the neonatal clinic in Springfield, Missouri. I followed in our car. At the Harrison hospital, the male doctor continued to rant at Luisa, who drifted in and out of consciousness as Lola stood by, unable to stop him.

Luisa recovered quickly. Mario did too.

But Mario would be the only little Spirit we brought into this world together.

Everyone loved Mario. Even the locals. Even before he was born. Late in Luisa's pregnancy, a goat and milk cow farmer we had worked for part-time, by the name of Don Sigmon, stopped by with an apartment-scale propane stove range and a propane tank. "Y'all can't be having no stove with a baby coming," he said. We still cooked over a campfire in 1987.

Even before that, things had begun to thaw a little with some of the locals in the valley. It started with the Villines family. The father, the elder, stayed standoffish, but his son Paul, who is my age, came up here with a backhoe to put our spring in. Later Paul hired us to work the cattle at a certain time of year, when they took their shots. Nobody else in those parts would give us a job.

Babies and puppies, though, soften the hardest of hearts. In our case, it was a horse rather than a puppy who first helped some locals along. Nightdancer—my tall, high-spirited, gray-dappled Appaloosa mare— ranged freely unless I called her for a ride. When I rode her off the land— wearing my jeans and tee shirt, belt with buck knife, cowboy boots, and big, black Stetson hat with a brightly beaded headband—folks noticed us. While adults either hailed or ignored us on the road, children could not resist us. "What's the horse's name?" "Can we pet her?" "Are you an Indian?" "Can I get on Nightdancer?" I would let them mount for a minute if their parents allowed it. Sometimes I'd deliver small care packages of home-made gingerbread cookies to Nightdancer's little admirers. Hearts thawed a bit more.

Then when we stopped by with Mario, a cute, fat, little Indian baby strapped to a cradleboard, those hearts melted outright. "He is a dandy. Can I hold him? Can I hold him?" Everyone had to see him, a boy born to the world! People who had avoided us for years began to acknowledge us.

From the very start, Mario absorbed the natural world around him. When he was a couple of months old, we propped him up against a tree in his cradleboard. He looked around while we worked in the garden. He watched butterflies and gazed at the leaves trembling in the breeze and turned knowingly to the birds' calls. He seldom cried.

Later, with an active toddler on our hands, we created an open-air playpen for him. As soon as he could understand the rules, we fenced in three acres around the house, sectioning off the pond and other potential hazards. We instructed him to stay inside the fence and answer when we called, because we were not able to see him at all times.

Mario spent his early days outside in the yard or down at the swimming hole with us, even hiking through the gorge with us on his strong little legs. Insects and animals amused him. From a young age, he would pick up the tiniest bug to show us its unique features—a translucent wing, a spotted leg. He managed to get himself inside a small cage, about two feet tall and three feet across, with a mother hen and her chicks, who climbed all over him as if he too were their mother. He would roll around on the ground with the cats and lie out in the sun with the dogs, one of the pack. Gradually, as he got older, he learned the wild plants, what to forage and what to leave in peace. In later years, we dubbed him the Mushroom Man when he brought delicious, edible varieties to our table: morel, puffball, oyster, chicken of the woods, cock's comb, lion's mane . . .

♪ ♪ ♪

Luisa, however, had fallen into profound depression, no run-of-the-mill postpartum blues, soon after Mario's birth. Trauma so deep, so bound up in racism and homophobia, pulls up old wounds as it creates fresh ones. Nobody could have bounced gleefully into motherhood after the treatment Luisa suffered from midwife and medical doctor alike. At first, she would not let Mario from her sight. Then she turned on me. I had done all in my power to help her birth our baby safely. I knew she knew that, but her rage and terror had to go somewhere.

When Mario was about a year and a half old, Luisa decided to get a job on the line at a factory some towns over. She became more and more distant from me as the months went by, often taking Mario with her to stay in town for days or weeks at a time.

I then descended into a deep depression of my own, which lasted more than a year. I could not shake it and I could not bear it.

Finally, when Mario was about three years old, I called Elena Avila, a curandera who had mentored me for some time. "I can't do this anymore, Elena. I want to die. Or can I come to you? Help me find myself again."

"Come on out here," Elena said. She was a psychiatric nurse as well as a curandera, healing those who sought her out in New Mexico.

Just before I departed, Luisa decided that she needed me after all. She begged me to stay.

"It's too late, Luisa. If I stay here, I will die. I am done."

She cried and pleaded. Finally, she said, "Then we'll come with you." She talked me into it.

We found people to foster our animals. Our herd of six milk goats went to one family, rabbits and chickens and turkeys to others. Another friend put our horses out in his pasture. We had already given up our donkey, who had become territorial and jealous after Mario's birth. We closed up the house. With no other women living here at that time, Jenny having moved to Fayetteville with some friends, we just shut the place down.

My brother Jesús had a studio in an old adobe school building in Cerrillos, about thirty minutes from Elena's place. Luisa, Mario, and I moved into an apartment in the school building. Jesús hired Luisa to do some carpentry work for him, while I touched up the beautiful carved paintings, traditional petroglyphs, which wound around the structure's facades. As he had done for other members of la familia at his primary workshop in Rockport, Jesús drew us into his monumental success as a sculptor of granite. He understood our need and gave us work to suit our skills.

Though I had gone there for Elena to heal me, our arrangement turned out to be reciprocal, as messed up as I felt when I arrived there. "What you have done, what you are doing, surpasses anything I have been around," Elena said. "What you're trying to do is considered impossible, to reclaim the medicine in the hostile environment of Arkansas and with so many obstacles, the isolation you as women of color endure there. Will you share your medicine with us here?"

I asked permission to build a lodge there on the property Jesús owned, an adobe lodge, which is more traditional to that area. We started conducting women's lodge Ceremonies with Elena and her group of apprentices. Word spread. Women came from Santa Fe and Albuquerque to see me and get treatments. Many came for Ceremony.

Still I struggled to recover joy in my life. Seeing that, Elena invited me to study in Peru with her, all expenses paid, under the direction of the chamán Eduardo Calderón. "I think this is what you need," she said.

At the last minute, Elena decided not to go. She had a premonition of her own death if she went there. I ended up going alone, first to Lima, where I stayed with a physician and his wife, friends of Elena.

No one had warned me that at that time civil war raged in the inland area of Peru where Calderón lived, with power and phone lines going out from random small bombings and extreme caution urged for tourists, who made easy high-profile targets. I stood out like a sore thumb, towering over the average Peruvian by a full head or more. Nevertheless, I survived the period of study with Calderón, returning from his inland retreat to Lima mostly disappointed by the patriarchal, chauvinistic ego this famous chamán displayed.

A message awaited me on my return to the city, from another chamán, originally from Bolivia, living currently in Peru with his son. Froilan Monzon Zegarra. The doctor's wife told me that Froilan had asked her to bring me to him. "He healed me when I had a miscarriage and couldn't come out of the postpartum depression," she told me. "He saved my life. Now he wants to meet you. He asked me for you."

"Did you tell him about me?"

"I said nothing at all."

I went to meet him. He had psychic abilities, as some chamánes do. He told me about my past and he told me about my future. He taught me the Mesa Ceremony, and I gathered my own healing from him. Then he said, "You don't have enough money to go home. They charge you a tariff to leave. So, I have arranged a healing for you, of a doctor who has been bewitched. I know you can do it."

I held a powerful Mesa Ceremony on the full moon for the doctor, who thanked me profusely for the medicine and paid me $200.

On parting, Froilan said, "I want you to know that you are a young chamán. You must remember who you are. You must continue on this path. And one more thing. You should not go back to that woman. She will only cause you pain."

I obeyed his direction in the years to come, working on myself as a healer, sharpening my skills as a chamán. I also disobeyed his direction, throwing myself back into the life Luisa and I had built together with renewed hope and commitment.

14

Back to the Land

In 1993, the state of Arkansas decreed that anyone practicing massage therapy needed a license. While I could have stayed under the radar practicing from the land, I heard the call from Latino activists throughout Northwest Arkansas for a traditional healer, a curandera, to serve our people. Many had sought me out by that time for healing. To extend my reach into the city, I would need the state's stamp of approval to put my hands on people, and the deadline to be grandfathered in had just passed.

Massage school, which I attended in Fayetteville, challenged me in new ways. I had not been in a formal school setting for many years, except for an art class and a computer class at the local community college. The different massage modalities presented in the program resembled work I had been doing for years already; that part came easily. The college-level anatomy and physiology classes, with all the terminology, required a different kind of focus. But life had thrown greater obstacles in my path. I doubled down on the books and earned the license. For the first time, in 1994, I could hang out my shingle.

Once I got my license, the stream of people who came to me for healing surged into a river. Word of mouth served as my only advertisement. I first took a job at the Fayetteville Athletic Club as a massage therapist, with the intention of gathering clientele. Word of my initial licensed employment spread. Four months later, when I had saved up enough money to rent office space and buy waiting-room furniture, I opened my own practice in Fayetteville, often seeing as many as eight clients a day, Monday through Friday.

Luisa, too, had returned to school, first at the community college and then at the university. We patched together a city-country arrangement for a couple of years in all, as we each got schooled and launched in our respective "licensed" careers. During the week, we stayed in a small rented house in Fayetteville, where Mario also went to school. On the weekends, we returned home to the land.

✦ ✦ ✦

I lasted a year in private practice in town. It wore me out. Clients, more of them than I could handle, crowded my schedule and my consciousness. I needed a break. "I'm moving back to the mountain," I told people. "If you want badly enough to see me, you will find your way there." They did. Plus, I made selected house calls to steady clients in Northwest Arkansas; these folks paid top dollar and a tip. The plan brought in good money with no overhead.

A few years earlier, an activist group from Boston had come to help us build a barn on the land. In that structure, we had housed our horses, donkey, goats, rabbits, turkeys, and chickens. Then, during Luisa's pregnancy, we had added a second story to the building, to be used as a bunkhouse for people staying on the land. Now that we finally had some money saved, we could complete the wiring in the building and turn part of the second floor into my workspace, which we named, simply, La Clínica. The addition of a long-range antenna telephone further enabled me to operate my practice from our remote location, as did power generated by solar panels.

Over our many years on the land, we had worked on the infrastructure as funds and labor allowed. In the earliest years, that meant clearing trees to open trails from Sassafras to Arco Iris. Later we cleared flat land spaces as we built various structures and gardens. Road improvement and maintenance began in 1976 and continues to this day, as we clear our dirt road of fallen trees, fill in ruts caused by heavy weather, and clean debris from gutters and culverts up and down our three-mile stretch.

As early as 1978, we paid to have a half-acre pond (later enlarged to a full acre) dug with a backhoe. We stocked it with fish. Turtles, frogs, and birds soon made their way there. Deer and their fawns came to drink, especially in the dry season. We not only swam in the clear, spring-fed pond but also installed an underground water line from there to our garden, irrigating the plot with the nutrient-rich pond water.

A few years later, we built a nine-hundred-gallon cistern for rainwater catchment off the house. Luisa and I, by ourselves, hand dug a seven-foot-deep and seven-foot-wide hole, built a form, and hand poured a concrete floor and wall. After installing a hand pump, we could use the water collected in our cistern for dishes, for the animals, and for washing up in general.

Before Mario's birth, we developed a spring high above our homestead to run a water line directly to our farm, bringing spring water to our house through natural gravity flow. Don Sigmon, who had brought us our first propane stove, also delivered to us by tractor a three-hundred-gallon steel milk tank. He hauled it all the way from his farm in Berryville, thirty-five miles away, for us to repurpose as a water tank.

Bit by bit, we built structures on the land, those for everyday life and those for Ceremony: our own home, Jenny's cabin, Mario's cabin, the roundhouse, a large pavilion and outdoor kitchen, the Crystal Medicine Wheel. Later we added a few prefabricated cabins, which we then expanded and improved, bringing solar-generated power and spring water to some, as funds allowed.

With every change we made on the land, I savored the continuities of our lives here even more. From my first day here, and at the start of each day since, I have sought to meet the dawn with prayer. I speak each day to Huehueteotl, God of Fire, creator of life and death. I sit with this old god of great wisdom and I see our likeness, the fire that burns within us, a fire that must be tended and stoked, thanked for every moment of life and revered in Ceremony. Nothing separates the sacred and the ordinary here. Work is not limited to a 9-to-5 schedule; prayers of gratitude and introspection cannot be contained by clock or calendar. You do not have a day off when you live on the land, just as you do not have time off when you live in Spirit, grounded in nature and Her seasons: In spring, we plant our garden and in summer we reap the harvest; in fall we cut and stack firewood and in winter we haul it inside to keep the fire going. As our Ancestors lived, we seek to live.

Make no mistake: We worked constantly on the land, from the first day forward. If labor defines farm life, it double defines wilderness life. Visitors came and went; clients checked in and out of my busy Clínica. Yes, we took time to celebrate special occasions, the yearly traditions of our peoples, gathering to greet the Ancestors on El Día de los Muertos, celebrating the harvest on Thanksgiving, rolling dozens upon dozens of tamales at Christmas. But through it all, then as now, work never left. It preceded, accompanied, and followed all else, constant and steadying, sacred as a prayer.

And even though Luisa would eventually leave the land, and leave me, as Chamán Froilan had predicted, I credit her always with almost thirty years of hardworking dedication to the life we built together. We lived a purposeful life, day after day, month after month, year after year, and most especially, season after season, each in its turn, each a marker on our spiritual path.

In this sacred place, all work gives birth to life. In our wilderness medicine wheel sanctuary, all labor sustains our Indigenous ways. Here, nestled deep in the forest on our Mother Earth, we lend all of our energy to healing ourselves and others, that we may see the Way. None is less holy than the next: meditating, mucking animal pens, performing Ceremony, milking goats, planting our garden in spring, gathering herbs, cutting firewood, praying, emptying compost toilets, blessing the land, dumping ashes, smudging, feeding farm animals, healing the sick, gathering eggs, relocating venomous snakes, hunting deer . . . All is sacred in this place.

In late spring, soon after Mario turned twelve years old, we prepared him for his coming-of-age Vision Quest with a Purification Ceremony. Luisa and I prayed and sweat with him in the lodge, within yards of his place of birth, on the land he knew as his own Mother.

We then walked with him far away, across three bluffs, to our Vision Spot. Luisa and I carried the water, the buffalo robe, the medicine pouch, and the medicine pipe. "We carry these things for you, son, because you are still a boy. When you come back, you will carry them, because then you will be a man." We set up a protected space with tobacco ties surrounding it and left him alone there for two days, wearing only a breechcloth. He had one pint of water, no food, and no shelter, only the buffalo robe for comfort or cover. He would stay there and pray for a vision. We would return for him at high noon, in two days.

Mario never voiced any fear. Calm and serious, he seemed to know the significance of this Ceremony of Transition. He trusted Mother Nature to care for him. So did we, though he looked small and young, still a child, as we left him on his Quest.

On the second day, la familia and friends came to welcome him home. They brought food and gifts to honor his journey into manhood. On that day, we prepared the lodge to receive him.

Just as Luisa and I set out to escort him back from the Vision Spot, Mario appeared at our clearing, bearing the empty water bottle, the buffalo robe, the medicine pouch, and the medicine pipe. Covered in bites, and looking small and tired, he appeared shocked when we all cheered his arrival. He had not understood that we would come to escort him home from the bluff.

Luisa and I immediately took him into the Ceremonial lodge to share his experience with us, only us. Then he washed and dressed in clean, nice clothes. We all feasted and presented gifts to him, as is tradition.

We swelled with pride for our son, who after fasting for two days had carried a heavy load unassisted across three bluffs to join us in Ceremony. "You have demonstrated your inner strength and courage," I said. "You have become a man."

15

Heartbreak and Healing

More often in my life than I can put to coincidence, I have witnessed tragedy followed by transformation, by an opening of possibility. At times, I have seen this only in hindsight. Other times, I have sensed the momentum of events as if in a lucid dream, awake and asleep all at once, aware on multiple levels. So it was when my much-loved friend and Jenny's god-mother, Marsha Gómez, died and Arco Iris came into stewardship of our sister mountain—where Sassafras had bloomed and faltered, where I had died and been reborn as SunHawk many years before.

Marsha and her lover Clary Pérez had lived at Sassafras for several years, in a cabin they named La Salsa. Always clear-sighted about where the power structure lay, Marsha maintained relations with the white women over there through it all; she tried to have allies on all sides, white and brown and Black. Eventually she moved to Austin, where she helped found the Indigenous Women's Network, along with a local arts organization, Artistas Indigenas, and finally the nonprofit Alma de Mujer Center for Social Change. She lived her dreams as a sculptor, potter, activist, and Ceremonial leader, sometimes with funding from the white Texas oil heiress and feminist philanthropist Genevieve Vaughan, who commissioned what would become Marsha's most famous sculpture, *Madre Del Mundo*.

In the *Madre* sculpture, an Indigenous woman sits cross-legged. Her head tilts down. A globe rests on her lap like a pregnant belly or a child just born. One hand cradles its curved edges; the other rests lightly on her own thigh. Rays of connection between mother and child stream from this larger-than-life-sized mother/goddess, which Marsha replicated several times after the 1988 original moved many hearts toward our Mother Earth.

When Marsha's adult son, who had been diagnosed with schizophrenia, got charged with her murder, all of us felt our own hearts ripped open in ways we could never have imagined. I wonder to this day about Mekaya's conviction, based on circumstantial evidence, and about his death from "unknown causes" in prison three years later.

Marsha's death slammed us all hard—in Texas, in Arkansas, across the continental US, and into our communities in Hawai'i and Mexico and Canada. I was in California when word of her death came, staying with my friend Celia Rodríguez and her partner, Cherríe Moraga, in Oakland. Creative artists, academics, and activists in the Latina lesbian community, Celia and Cherríe knew and loved Marsha dearly. Celia, as a curandera and Ceremonial leader, understood, as I did, that we had to step up immediately to assist Marsha's Spirit in its transition. When someone dies tragically, their Spirit must not be left out in limbo, where it can get trapped by the trauma of the death itself. As Marsha's Spirit Keeper, I would hold her close for a full year, to help her Spirit find its way clear from the trauma of a violent transition from this life. In the immediate aftermath, however, we prepared an altar with Marsha's picture displayed on it. We prayed for her Spirit. We prayed for our own strength to face the tragedy that had befallen our sister and our community. We prayed out enough of our grief to be able to move and function, and then we caught a flight to Austin.

Celia and I went together to Marsha's home to clean the energy and pray with Marsha's Spirit to gather strength for her final passage. We understood that you have to talk to the Spirit, bathe it in words and prayers and smoke, reassure the Spirit so that it can let go and move on. Marsha's body had already been removed and cared for by the local women, to be cremated. We worked to heal her Spirit.

People came from all over the world, on short notice, to say goodbye to Marsha. We met for Ceremony at Alma de Mujer to honor her. To be in the company of many others who loved and cherished my dear sister—a warrioress like few others—helped my heart as much as it could be helped right then.

When I returned home, I felt the weight of sorrow on the women here in Northwest Arkansas. I decided to hold a memorial for Marsha on the land.

Soon after I put word out to the women's community, Diana Rivers contacted me to ask if she could attend. She had not been here on the land in all those years. "If you come in peace," I said. "This is a Ceremony where we can share our grief and our prayers together."

The Earth here speaks to me. On the day of the memorial, She spoke clearly: Hear me, She said. *Walk to the bluff.*

Jenny and I left the gathering of women planting clumps of bulbs in Marsha's memory across our clearing. We walked to the high bluff. We had stood on that lookout point countless times over the years, facing toward Marsha and Clary's cabin at Sassafras, La Salsa, which even on the barest day of winter could not be glimpsed through the trees.

A storm had recently ripped through our mountains, winding its way up from Austin with torrents of rain, bringing hail and a powerful tornado. It had begun the night we left Marsha's funeral in Austin, preceding us by some hours. We stopped in Dallas to call the Newton County officials, surmising correctly that our road would be impassable; they cleared the way for us as best they could, and as quickly.

Now, standing on the high bluff, Jenny and I saw the full results of the tornado. It had cut a path, clear and distinguished, with hundreds of downed trees leaving a corridor from our bluff to Sassafras, where we could now see La Salsa. Marsha's Spirit had spoken: *These lands are connected. Honor that path.*

As I emerged from the lodge after leading Ceremony, someone called me into the house to take a phone call. A white lesbian friend of mine from the nearby town of Jasper spoke in a panic. "SunHawk! Somebody is trying to quiet the title for your land. That means they're trying to take it away from you!"

"Who would do that?"

"It says Diana Rivers. I saw the notice in the newspaper."

"How could that be? Diana is here now, on the land. She came in peace." I thought for a moment, and then it hit me. "How much land? What does it say?"

"Four hundred acres."

"That's Sassafras!"

I said nothing to Diana that day. I never move impulsively on matters of importance. I await further instruction. I await clarity. I pray for direction. I do a lot of Ceremony.

Luisa and I discussed it all, at length: What was Diana planning to do with the land if she got the others off the deed? Was she going to sell it? Would her sons someday inherit it and sell it to developers? Already, the locals had been hunting and looting and poaching and partying on the abandoned land, shooting up the place. We worried about stray bullets, and we feared the consequences of an outright sale of the four-hundred-acre expanse that had once been paired with our sacred land.

We decided, since Diana had asked permission to come and be at my home for Marsha's memorial, that I could ask permission to speak to her about the Sassafras land. We set up a meeting to talk at her house in Fayetteville.

In the meantime, I called Shiner in California. She remained the sole member of the Sassafras collective who had not signed off on her claim to the land. If she did not respond to the newspaper notice quieting the title, the land would go by default to Diana after thirty days. "You have to come back here to help figure out what's best to happen with Sassafras. Things are not good over there. They're looting and trashing the place," I said.

"I can't get away right now," Shiner said. "Besides, you're the best one to decide what's to happen with the land." She had her lawyer draw up papers to give me power of attorney in the matter.

Once again, Diana and I would go head-to-head over the land.

On the way to Fayetteville, Luisa drove, as usual. I still did not know what exactly I would say to Diana. I knew that I wanted to protect the land. I knew that Marsha's Spirit had pronounced on the matter, clearing a visual path from Arco Iris to Sassafras. Jenny and I had borne witness to that miracle on the bluff. I prayed: *Guide me. What am I supposed to do? What are we supposed to do here?*

🖋 🖋 🖋

Diana seemed nervous, full of agitated motion, as her partner, Path, sat with Luisa and me in a quiet circle in her in-town home waiting to discuss the land.

"What do you plan to do with it?" I asked. "It has been abandoned for so many years." I spoke of our concerns on this side of the sister mountains.

"I just want to protect the land. I just want to protect it." She kept saying that, like a mantra.

The words tumbled out of me then. "Well, why don't you put all the land into Arco Iris? Put it into our nonprofit." We could come up with agreements about what we wanted for the land. Diana and Path could be on the board. We would call it Wild Magnolia, after the trees that colored the mountain each spring in wild, white-blossomed display.

To my amazement, Diana agreed.

❧ ❧ ❧

Arco Iris Vision Statement for Wild Magnolia

This sacred land will be a sanctuary for native plants and trees, wild animals, ecosystems, springs, creeks, caves, and people.

This sacred land will be cared for and protected by our community as a land trust held in perpetuity for future generations.

This land will have a resident gatekeeper who is honest, open, welcoming to well-intentioned visitors, yet aware and firm and physically capable of maintaining land regulations.

This sacred land will be physically and spiritually cleansed of old debris.

This sacred land will have at least three resident caretakers and/or families.

This sacred land will be shared with community and the public (eco-tours, Earth School, natural health clinic, retreats, ceremonies).

This sacred land is committed to diverse usage and diverse residents and visitors—female, male, LGBTQI folks, elders, children, people of color, and differently abled.

This land will provide a sacred and safe retreat area to be reserved as women-only space.

This sacred land will always share gardens, wildlife and fauna, and pasture areas with its founding neighbor's community, Arco Iris.

This sacred land space will have a suspension bridge that links the Arco Iris community with the Wild Magnolia community.

This sacred land will be the home of Teopan Earth School for the purpose of sustainability, to sustain Wild Magnolia and our Ozark rural community.

❡ ❡ ❡

Diana and I had been at odds for too long. To start anew in peace and sisterhood, Luisa and I invited her and Path out to the land for a "Bury the Hatchet Ceremony," which I created for the occasion.

We sat in a circle as I said an opening prayer. Each of us in turn then held the talking stick—a gift from Grandmother Cedar—to speak about our lives. High points, low points, trauma, healing. We shared what we needed, deep within ourselves, to work together for the land. The others listened without interrupting as each spoke from the innermost place of truth she could reach. We listened through the others' ears, saw through the others' eyes, drew breath through the others' lungs. As different as our lives had been, we had all known hardship and joy. We had taken risks and suffered losses. We had loved and sought comfort. When we listened with compassion, we sensed our common cause. We could bury the rusted old hatchet in the name of our Mother and our children, and for the future.

Tentatively at first, Diana ventured into the Arco Iris circle. She even began to join our annual Caminata, the Ceremony we had initiated in 1983, walking all the boundaries of the land to the highest point.

❡ ❡ ❡

Shiner had hoped to move back to the land someday. Fate had other plans for her.

She had been back to Arco Iris when her older son was around three years old. After that, we fell out of touch for a few years, until one fall, when I had gone out to California to get away from the land during allergy season, we had a chance encounter in the Mission District of San Francisco.

My friend Celia Rodriguez, who had a position at the time as director of the Latino museum there, invited me to attend a *folklorista*'s presentation of Mexican lore one afternoon. A woman with a young child sat beside me, settling in after the story had begun. Next thing I knew, she had placed her hand on mine. "Is it really you?" she whispered. "I see you everywhere, but it's never really you."

Shiner, with a second beautiful boy on her lap, reached over to embrace me.

We never lost touch again after that. I would stay with her in the Mission District on my allergy-season trips to the West Coast. She rode her bike to work at a sex toy warehouse run by a feminist collective there and lived alone with her two sons, Clay and Leo, who occupied every corner of her heart. We celebrated our Libra birthdays together several years running.

She wanted to visit us again more than ever after Diana ceded the old Sassafras land to Arco Iris. Then pancreatic cancer, stealthy and later brutal, came to claim her life at the age of forty-seven.

Toward the end, as I planned a final trip to see Shiner in this lifetime, I had a bad accident on the land. My truck rolled over me, breaking my leg and banging me up pretty good. I could not travel. In fact, the curandera Doña Enriqueta Contreras, who chewed me out for coming to Austin to consult her while I was still healing, forbade me to travel in my weakened condition. When Shiner called me in her final days, I could not go to her.

On her last day of life, she called me. She had asked her family—her parents, sister, brothers, ex-husband, and two sons—to sit her up in the bed, in lotus position, before they left the room to allow her space to talk freely. We talked for some time. She sounded lucid and intentional.

"I'm not a 'fraidy cat anymore," she said, referring to her abrupt departure from Sassafras when I lay dying of hepatitis many years earlier. She had become a Buddhist. "I'm ready."

I could not release her; I could not let go.

"Don't worry. I'm going to come back. Just call me and I will come. I am not afraid, SunHawk."

We prayed together. We said goodbye.

When her family came back in to check on her, they found her still in the lotus position. She had passed.

I do call her, often, and she returns. Tough, kind, gentle woman of my heart.

16

Águila

When Señora Cobb bestowed the title "Águila" on me, she gave me both a gift and a burden. Bear with me through the telling. This is a medicine story.

My friend Celia Rodriguez first introduced me to Señora Cobb. "You must meet her," Celia said. "She wants to meet you."

We arrived at Señora Cobb's modest, two-story wooden home in Sacramento to find her on the phone. Celia had to return immediately to Berkeley to teach a class. She waved a quick goodbye as my host pointed me toward a chair. "I told you I need this medicine bag ready for the Ceremony. I need the bag soon to go. The Ceremony is in a week," the señora said into the telephone, in distress.

As I sat there listening, my medicine bag came to mind. It is a leather bag, six inches wide and two feet long, its base crafted originally by a Native American woman incarcerated for defending herself against her abuser and given to me when I first moved out to the land. After years of my own Spirit-led embellishment, the plain leather piece now has beadwork winding around its base, painting a vision in symbols. A rainbow dominates the scene, connecting all of life to Spirit. Behind that, pyramids rise to represent sacred knowledge. Fertility symbols appear as water. And I, SunHawk, am a bird with broad wingspan, flying close to our Father Sun. It is a total medicine piece.

"I have the medicine bag you need," I said when she hung up the phone. "I left it at Celia's. You will have it to take to the Ceremony."

She asked no further questions of me, instead showing me around her house, talking all the while of her astonishing life journey. She had been selected from her small Mexican village in the eastern Sierra Madre mountains as a child, the youngest of a group handpicked by a government-endorsed program to represent their regions' customs and ceremonies, and especially their songs and dances, under the direction of the legendary Danza Azteca teacher Florencio Yescas. The children lived together, receiving tutoring and eventually education through college or university, as they traveled first throughout Mexico and then internationally, demonstrating the original sacred ways of the Indigenous people through dance and song. Angelbertha, whose Nahuatl name, Ixchel, means *arco iris*, or "rainbow," landed eventually in Sacramento, California, with Earl Cobb, the first of the two husbands she would outlive. She birthed nineteen children and taught them the dances and rituals of her people. Over many decades, Señora Cobb became the West Coast leader of the Danza Azteca movement in the US, as she performed and educated one generation after another in the pre-invasion ways of the Indigenous México people. Cultural ambassador, social justice activist, mother, dancer, teacher, and professor all rolled into one, she served in practice as a spiritual and Ceremonial leader for those who could perceive her powers.

Each room of her house felt like a museum, crammed with the regalia and artifacts of her long life: walls covered with the plaques and awards she had received in appreciation of her civic work; display after display of the feathered, beaded, brightly colored headpieces, dresses, and other costumes of the dancers; and Florencio Yescas's magnificent throne, gilded and covered with jaguar skin, which the Azteca dancers carry on their shoulders in their rituals. I had never been in such a place. There might not be another like it.

Yet Señora Cobb remained humble. She spoke in a direct manner. No pretensions. After Celia brought her the medicine bag, Señora Cobb later told me, she had examined it closely, turning it over and over to understand its meaning. "I was going to a Ceremony for *chamánes*, all women. It was to be held at a pyramid site, a sacred site outside Mexico City, just as you depicted on the bag. I knew it was a powerful medicine bag. I knew I must bring it with me."

/ / /

When I next saw Señora Cobb, about a year later, she pressed an object into my palm. It felt cool and hard, fitting perfectly into the cradle of my left hand, which she wrapped in her own two hands as she told me the fate of my medicine bag.

"I knew I had to protect that sacred piece at the Ceremony," she said. "I covered it with my rebozo the whole time I was in the procession to the meeting."

As an elder, she was seated in the front. The head priestess immediately pointed to her. "Come here, come here." Señora Cobb made her way forward.

"Uncover that bag," the priestess said. "Bring that bag to me. Hand it to me. This bag belongs here. It is a part of this Ceremony. The maker of this bag will be honored. She will be acknowledged." Señora Cobb handed the bag to the priestess, who placed it on the altar.

As she left the Ceremony, the señora passed through the usual line of vendors selling replicas of artifacts—obsidian knives, sacred pipes, gods and goddesses made of jade—as well as incense, copal, and other items used for Ceremony. Her apprentice, being a male, coveted an obsidian knife, a replica of one used in Ceremony by some shamans. She bought it for him, along with a few other small gift items, replicas of artifacts. All of these she put in her own bag before she proceeded with the others to the grand plaza of the cathedral the Spanish had built over an Indigenous sacred site, after enslaving the Indians.

From the corner of her eye as she stood on the plaza talking to old friends, she saw two ancient people dressed in white, a woman and a man. Suddenly they appeared at her side. The woman pressed a small object into her hand. "Take this to the maker," the old woman said. "Hide it quickly." As they vanished back into the crowd, Señora Cobb deftly stuffed the object deep inside her bra.

Just then a government agent came up to her. "Do you have any artifacts? You know you're not supposed to sell or get heritage artifacts?" He made her show him the contents of her bag. All replicas, nothing important.

When she got back to her room, she fished the object out from her bosom. A jade god, like a god's head. An artifact. Real, and very old. It fit perfectly in the palm of her hand. She did not know what it signified. She did know it was for me, in gratitude from the Ancestors for my medicine bag.

"Keep this safe," she said. "Someday the medicine bag will be returned to you."

* * *

Over the next several years, I made frequent visits to the West Coast. I offered workshops and did Ceremony and held impromptu clinics in Oakland, San Francisco, and Los Angeles. Many came to me for healing. Often on these sojourns out West, I drove to Sacramento to visit Señora Cobb.

At one point, after some years had passed, I paid Señora Cobb a visit. Luisa and I were in the throes of our final breakup. I felt like a leaden figure, struggling with each step as if a heavy load crushed my back. Back pain in fact kept me immobile at times; the body feels the Spirit.

"I cannot perform Ceremony anymore. It is too much," I told Señora Cobb. I had spoken to her before, many times, of my uneasiness in the role of Ceremonial leader. I had to push myself out there, always a reluctant leader, never one who glories in the role. "It is different now. I truly feel I cannot do it."

She left the room, returning several minutes later carrying a *penacho*, a headband that holds the feathers of a traditional headdress. "You have earned many eagle feathers. They have been gifted to you," she said. "Now you will gather all those feathers. You will place them into this penacho. It is time for you. It is time to take up your true place. It is time to take up your name. Now you are Águila."

I began to cry. She did not acknowledge my tears. She did not seek to comfort me.

"You are still flying too close to the Earth. You are weighted down. You must fly higher. You are the eagle. You are Águila. You have the ability to fly close to the sun, to receive the messages from the Creator. You can see from that high place. You will not be pulled down. You will not be scorched. You soar above. From where you fly, you see only beauty. *You are Águila!*"

I wept.

"From here on, you will wear the full headdress at Ceremony. I don't care if you don't want to. You will do it. This is not a whim. It is your sacred duty. You are Águila!"

✒ ✒ ✒

I was to wear the full headdress for the first time at our spring walk, our Caminata, that year. Sitting in our house as everyone waited at dawn for me in the roundhouse, I tried to gather my strength. I trembled. I meditated. I prayed. I sat bareheaded, eyeing the headdress. How could I face the group wearing that outlandish piece? Who was I to claim the name Águila? Was Señora Cobb mistaken? Her blessing felt more burden than gift.

I placed the feather-filled penacho on my head, as duty required.

Like the shot of Shakti from the touch of Swami Muktananda's peacock feather decades ago, the eagle feathers poured pure energy into me, suffusing my whole being with an electric peace, with all of the energies of the Universe melded into one force, intensely beautiful, transitory, seen from the eye of an eagle in flight. I felt all fear drain away. I began to walk, encircled by a calm illumination, to the roundhouse. Dear ones waited there, and Spirit led the way. I walked in beauty.

17

To the Womb of Our Mother

Three Owls calling
June 4, 2018, past midnight

They come
Sacred Eagles of the Night
Loud and demanding my presence

Knowingly, I light the cedar
I go out to them
Carrying my cedar burning

I pray,
Ozumare, Rainbow Medicine,
Feathered Serpent
Guardian Spirit
Keeper of sacred space
Sanctify me

They come
Loudly demanding my presence
They call again and again

They call loudly
Their eerie calls, over and over
Over and over

Perched in the oak tree above me
The Great Eagle of the East
Eagle of the Night Sky
Illuminator of darkness
She calls loudly
Demanding my presence

I come to Her
Yet my eyes cannot see
In the darkness of the night
I ask, Illuminate me

She speaks again loudly
I speak back, in my best calls
Again She speaks in the East,
Then another in the South,
And another to the West
Then others further away
They call out loudly,
One then another
Then all at once, all together
Again and again they call back and forth

I speak back, in my best calls
Honoring each as they speak in turn to me

I cannot see them
In the darkness of the night
Nor can I understand their tongue
Yet, we talk and talk, until I grow weary

I wait for the Great One of the North
I wait but She does not call
Did She not come?
I wait for the Great One of the North
Keeper of knowledge and wisdom
Eagle of the Night Sky
But it is late
And I grow weary

Great One of the North bring me Knowledge
Night Eagle, Keeper of the Night Sky
Great One of the North bring me Wisdom
Of the unseen, of what is yet to come

Weary, I retreat
I go to my nest to sleep
Insistently they continue to speak
Loudly demanding they call
Loudly demanding they call
That I remember our time
Remember my purpose

Wearily, I go to sleep, to dream,
That I might then understand

All knowing, they come
To teach me
Stay awake even in your dream
Stay present,
Keep ready, keep centered
Be present
Even in your dream

Walk in power
Be not afraid
We are with/in you.

—María Cristina Moroles / Águila

Luisa left in 2011. I will not tell that story here.

After she left, I began to call the land "Santuario Arco Iris." Called "Rainbow Land" originally, and then "Rancho Arco Iris" for a spell when we had horses, this sacred refuge needed a new name. I needed a sanctuary, more than ever before. The land came into its truest title at my moment of greatest despair. Santuario Arco Iris has never failed to live up to its promise.

✦ ✦ ✦

In 2015, Jesús died in a car accident in Jarrell, Texas. Though he had been unwell, suffering from silicosis from years of inhaling dust from the granite he sculpted into massive, abstract works that reside as far away as the Great Wall of China and as close by as the plaza of the law school at the University of Arkansas in Fayetteville, his abrupt transition pierced la familia with wounds we still seek to heal. I became the eldest of the surviving Moroles siblings, a role I never wanted, a role I pray to bear with dignity.

Mi familia gave me the honor of leading the opening Ceremony at the memorial for my brother, at the site of his largest sculpture, the Houston Police Officers' Memorial. His artwork dots the Earth, from New York City to Houston to Egypt and China and many locations in between. Art critics have called him a "shaman of stones." He was also, and foremost, a good son, father, brother, and man. Jesús Moroles has joined the Ancestors.

✦ ✦ ✦

And then, on December 20, 2017, Mom left this life. I spoke her eulogy:

> How can I honor in words this great woman who was a good daughter, sister, wife, mother, and grandmother? Words can neither encompass nor express our Spirit. I will do my best to share with you some few important facts about my mother, María Bautista Moroles, the spiritual matriarch of our family. . . .

Mom left no granite monuments, few objects of material value, no fame beyond la familia. She lived a humble life this time through. Yet unlike most who leave this life, she cannot now suddenly join the Ancestors: Mom *never left the Spirit world* as she sojourned here on Earth. A chamán of souls, a seer, a vidente, she walked in beauty every day of this life, into the next. Someday we will walk together again.

* * *

In the spring of 2018, Isis came to stay with me on the land. She had been calling me for months about one ailment or another. Her head hurt. She felt nauseous. Her smoker's cough had deepened. I would get medicine to her; she would get better for a spell. Then she would call again to say that the dis-ease had shifted to a new part of her body. She felt exhausted. Her equilibrium was off. She could no longer drive.

"I want you to come here," I said. "I need to observe you and treat you in person, over time."

She resisted. She enjoyed life in her tiny house. Increasingly messy over time, as disorganized as her mind, the space belonged to her alone. The piles of papers and mementoes reflected her many interests, her passions and wounds of a lifetime. At once an art studio and a library, a shrine to Princess and a photo gallery of babies Mama Bear had delivered during a turn as a midwife, as well as a repository for every unfiled piece of paper that had ever caught Isis's ever-shifting attention—the cabin had descended into chaos. We all feared the blaze that a cigarette or joint flicked in the wrong direction could spark. Isis felt rooted there, no matter what. She did not want to leave, even for a few weeks of my care.

Isis did not feel lonely or neglected living across the creek from the OLHA women, even as she understood full well the symbolism of the dividing line, the watery "railroad tracks." She got it at every level, from OLHA's buy-in fees to its bylaws. She got it, and she still felt connected to some of the women in that community.

Isis had become close in recent years to Nancy Vaughn, one of OLHA's old-timers. They made an unlikely pair, those two. Nancy's military background tilted her toward a more orderly take on the shape of a day or month or life. Isis, of course, marched and danced to her own inner beat only. But Goddess willing, we bend and grow when we are ready.

Nancy was bitten by a water moccasin a few years back. Of all the people who came to her aid—day after day, week after week, Isis stepped up. She brought the same red-hot devotion to Nancy's care as she had brought to her sacred fire keeping at Arco Iris. She showed up, and Nancy thanked her through countless small acts of gratitude: buying groceries, doing laundry, making repairs. Queen "Mama Bear" Isis Brown and Captain Nancy Vaughn, US Army (ret.), became besties.

Isis finally agreed to come here. We drove out to get her and moved her into the house with me. I tried everything in my arsenal to help her. She would get a little better, then fall into exhaustion and a resumption of symptoms: shape-shifting pain, a body-wracking cough, headaches, a lack of appetite, nausea, dizziness. She refused consultation with any Western medical doctor.

I called my friend Francesca, a Latina acupuncturist and doctor of Eastern traditional medicine in Eureka Springs. "May I bring Isis to you?" I asked. "It just keeps moving around. I can't figure out what it is. Maybe we can consult together?"

Isis consented. After a long examination, Francesca said, "You need to go to the emergency room. That is the best place, because they can do numerous tests right then and there."

"No way," Isis said. "I know how they treat us."

It took all the wits and wiles of two strong women healers to get Isis to relent. I brought her to the emergency room at Mercy Hospital in Berryville, where X-rays revealed tumors in her brain. This doctor, too, had to convince Isis of the urgency of her situation. "You need to go by ambulance to Washington Regional Hospital in Fayetteville. Car is too risky. If you have a seizure, you will both be in danger." She agreed to go, in part because her across-the-creek neighbor, Michael, practiced social work there.

An MRI revealed more. Brain cancer. Not operable. Terminal, with weeks or months to live.

Isis turned to me upon hearing the news. "I want you to be my medical person. You make the decisions on what is done. I don't want any extraordinary measures." We called Michael in for the paperwork to make that official.

"They're recommending hospice," I told her.

"No, I want to go to Nancy's."

I called Nancy, who said she would get it in the works when she returned from vacation in a week. At hospice in Fayetteville, Isis received medicine to reduce the inflammation, which also made her more lucid and as cantankerous as hell. I had to ride her about being so harsh with the nurses and doctors. "These people are here because they want to make you comfortable. Please, Isis. They have families. They have lives. They have feelings. Don't be so mean to them."

Before we left Fayetteville, she said, "I want you to document my death. Photograph it. It's important to me, and it's important for you."

"Important for me?"

"I know it will be. Promise me you'll document all the way, through to my burial."

"I promise I will."

When we arrived at Nancy's house, Isis announced, "SunHawk is in charge. Whatever she says goes."

Nancy had a large screened-in porch, surrounded like a nest by an arbor of hickory trees, with a maple and basswood thrown in. She had designed and built the house to flow into the hillside, to be part of nature. "This is where I want to stay," Isis said.

I wanted the porch to be cleared and cleaned out first, stripped of the various boxes, suitcases, furniture, and other objects that had accumulated there over the years. "Can we get some volunteers to come help?"

A young lesbian couple, carpentry students of Nancy's, came. Another young woman, a quiet friend to Isis, came. We cleaned the room from top to bottom before placing the bed supplied by hospice in the center, facing out into the lush green canopy beyond. I smudged the room and created beautiful altars on each side of the bed.

The porch now a sacred space, we brought Queen Isis out there. She looked around slowly, taking in every detail. "It is good" was all she said.

I asked hospice to come out to train us in the tender and dignified care of our sister Isis: how to bathe her without fumbling; how to toilet her without causing humiliation as she became less mobile; how to administer the medications they prescribed, and when.

Early in the sojourn from this life to the next, Isis and I spoke intimately about her transition. To the last detail, we decided together what would be done. She wanted only her medical marijuana for pain, until that became insufficient; only then did she want the morphine hospice had prescribed. She listed the friends and family to contact when she passed. She chose the colorful cotton tapestry for the shroud we would wrap around her body. We spoke about her final Ceremony. We talked about the burial she wanted: green, uncasketed, in the small cemetery on OLHA ground. We agreed on the photographer, Anh Đào Kolbe—our queer, Vietnamese, social justice compadre, who would come periodically, through to the end, to document the death and burial. Isis never flinched.

From her perch on the porch, she held court. A steady stream of friends came to spend time with her. Isis had won many hearts over the years, people who enjoyed her, learned from her, partied with her, and fought alongside her in the trenches of social justice warfare. Quite a few traveled from out of town—from California and the Northwest and as far out East as New York City—to say their goodbyes. Fayetteville community members made the pilgrimage to OLHA in sizeable numbers. Jenny, Mario, and other young people from our community came and sang to her, played music by her bed. Many others sent cards or called. Some sent food or money to help with her care. My dogs Django and Junko held vigil until Isis was not even aware of their presence anymore.

Some of the OLHA women came by. Diana and Path came, and a couple of others stopped by. Ironically, the most steadfast support came from a different women's land community, in Missouri; two elders, good friends of Isis's, moved into Nancy's house for several weeks to share round-the-clock duties with us. The four of us, with help from Jenny and a few others, served as the core crew.

I took care of the medicines we gave Isis until the very end, when she needed the morphine hospice had prescribed. My Shaman's Tea, various herbs, and CBD oil helped her to stay comfortable. I also made "canna-butter" from her medical marijuana, which I then dosed out to her in her food; and "herojuana," a thick resin made from the highest-quality cannabis buds, for pain relief, relaxation, and sleep. We figured out the scheduling holistically, through close observation and communication.

The core team of three women in their seventies and I did whatever needed to be done. We kept her clean. We kept her comfortable. As she became more fragile, our care became even more delicate. We bathed her in her bed. I oiled her skin and hair. We held her hand. We took shifts sleeping downstairs, close by, on alert. Near the end, she ceased speaking words. She moaned as the morphine wore off.

On the night she died, the pain seemed intense. Nancy, on duty that shift, tried to follow the morphine dosing instructions we had been given, to the minute. I could not bear it. I came downstairs. "We have to give her more medicine now," I said. "It's not right." I gave Isis another dose at around 3:00 a.m. She calmed and then she passed, at 3:30 a.m. on September 29, 2018.

✦ ✦ ✦

A green burial needs to happen quickly, within about thirty-six hours of death. We had planned every detail. We knew what to do, in what order. Nancy had prepared a phone tree, which included calls to Jenny to come out to help me prepare the body, to hospice to send someone out to confirm the death, and to Michael, across the creek, to bring dry ice to keep the body fresh through the hours of visitation before burial.

Hospice arrived quickly to pronounce Isis dead. Then Jenny and I washed and anointed her entire body with frankincense. I fixed her hair and oiled her braids. We wrapped her in the shroud she had chosen and placed her on a buffalo robe on fresh bedsheets, with her eagle feather resting on her chest, for visitors to come pay their respects.

Isis looked beautiful. She looked regal. She looked relaxed. Pain had contorted her face by the end. Now she smiled slightly, a radiant little goddess at rest.

We had not researched how much dry ice we needed. Michael brought an ice chest full of it. I arranged a layer beneath Isis, from head to legs.

Finally, Jenny went home and I went to bed. After an hour or so, Isis awakened me, grouchy as ever. "SunHawk," she called out. "I'm freezing!"

I ran downstairs to feel her body: almost frozen stiff. In a panic, I went online to find out how much dry ice we actually needed to use; it turned out to be about a third of what I had placed under her. Her body, which expanded as it froze, might explode. I called out to Nancy, "You've got to get up! We've got too much ice under Isis!"

With the extra ice stashed back in the cooler, Nancy and I trundled back to our beds, exhausted. "I'm good now," Isis told me. "I just didn't want you to make a big mess or make a fool of yourself."

✦ ✦ ✦

Visitors came throughout the day to pay their respects. With the funeral set for the morning of the next day, inside the thirty-six-hour window a natural burial requires, distant friends and family could not get there in time. Local friends stopped by with condolences, food, and flowers.

Aside from Diana, Path, and perhaps one other, the OLHA women did not come by. They continued with a planned workday in their garden, followed by a potluck. They did not pause. They did not come by with condolences or food for the women who had seen Isis through her transition.

* * *

In the morning, we gathered for the Ceremony. The pallbearers, dressed in black, included Nancy and the young woman down the hill, as well as Mario and other young people from our community. Isis lay wrapped in her cotton shroud, with the long, white drop cloth I had sewn placed beneath her body, on the pallet Nancy had crafted from sacred cedar wood.

The pallbearers lifted the cedar pallet reverently into the back of the cleaned-up truck we had designated as the hearse. They too sat in the truck's bed for the short drive down the hill, holding the cedar pallet still. At OLHA's fledgling cemetery, they positioned Isis over her burial spot, as the coroner stood to the side, head lowered in respect.

Those who could gathered around; several elders sat in chairs under a canopy tent. A child, now thirteen, whom Isis-as-midwife had delivered, stood with his mother. Mourners came from OLHA and they came from Fayetteville and they came from Eureka Springs. They came from the country and they came from the city. They came bearing flowers, which we placed near the freshly dug grave.

I opened the Ceremony, calling in the Spirits and Angels and Ancestors. I invited others to speak. Some shared stories of Isis. Our young people sang a homegoing hymn Isis loved.

We slipped the pallet out from under to lower the drop cloth, slowly, six feet down. There Isis would lie on the thick mattress of fresh green cedar boughs we had placed to cushion her.

We leaned, one by one, to place flowers in the grave.

There we left her, our Sister/Sistah Isis, deep in the womb of our Mother—atop a bed of sacred cedar, beneath a blanket of blossoms and leaves, violet and indigo, blue and green, yellow and orange and red—to join the Earth and the Ancestors.

Then we departed, a rainbow procession of Spirits on our long journeys home.

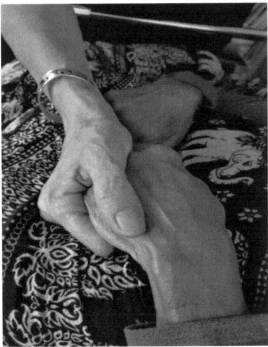

Courtesy Anh Đào Kolbe

Courtesy Anh Đào Kolbe

Courtesy Anh Đào Kolbe

18

Home

I am an Indigenous woman, a daughter of Tonantzin, my Mother Earth. I am a Two-Spirit Rainbow Prayer Warrior. I am Matriarch of Santuario Arco Iris, a wilderness healing sanctuary in the Ozark Mountains of Arkansas.

A vision led me to this land, with the sacred responsibility to protect my Mother Earth here in all Her aspects—Her water, soil, rock, and all inhabitants: trees, plants, animals, and all humans. As steward and spiritual leader and teacher, I follow the guidance of nature, my Mother Earth, my Ancestors, and the Ancestors of these lands. Dreams and visions of past, present, and future times guide me . . .

I approach my seventieth birthday this year, after nearly half a century on this mountain of my dreams and visions, my true home. Much has changed over the years and much remains the same.

🪶 🪶 🪶

Mi Querido Papá, Como Te Amo

Te amo por todo el Hombre que eres Hoy
Eres un Hombre Bueno
Eres un Hombre sabio
Eres un Hombre fuerte

Eres un Hombre noble
Y mas importante,
Eres un Hombre que sabe como Amar
Como amas a mi mamá, tu esposa, tu amiga, tu compañera
Como amas a tu familia, tus hijos, tu gente
Como amas a tu casa, tu jardin, tus plantas, las flores,
Como amas a todo la belleza de la vida
Gracias Papa por todo
Te amo para siempre,
Tu hija.

——*María Cristina Moroles / Águila*

My father, José Elizondo Moroles, joined the Ancestors on May 31, 2021, one day before his ninetieth birthday. His Spirit too has found its way home.

I felt his proud presence, and that of my mother, when the Sidney Lanier Elementary School in Dallas received a new name this year: the Jesús Moroles Expressive Arts Vanguard School. *Bueno,* Dad would say. *Como debe ser*—as it should be.

I believe that he and Mom would say the same of this mountaintop sanctuary, this land devoted to the ways of our Ancestors and the future of our people and planet. We are Rainbow Prayer Warriors, all.

Today on the land, I still live close to our Mother Earth, in a house built by women's hands, with power from the rays of our Father Sun and water from our mountain springs. Each morning as the sun rises, I step out of my house to pray in our Crystal Medicine Wheel. The garden still brings gifts. The forest still holds treasures. People still travel up our steep three-mile dirt road to La Clínica for help and healing. They come to our lodges, our medicine Ceremonies, and our annual Caminata. They attend our workshops and retreats on environmental education, sustainable living, Indigenous cultures, herbal healing, and more. They join our joyful celebrations and our mournful moments. Young people, most of them LGBTQI2S, spend weeks or months here as interns and apprentices, learning by doing, taking in the wisdom of our people in a simple and harmonious way. And still, women and children of color and displaced Indigenous peoples find their way here in times of need. Santuario Arco Iris remains a sanctuary, a refuge, a place of renewal and rebirth.

I still work hard, every day and every season. I still struggle for funds to complete the work entrusted to me through vision and prayer. I will never "sell" or debase our Mother simply to secure those funds. The land is protected in perpetuity, legally and spiritually, as the Arco Iris Earth Care Project, a nonprofit organization with stewards in residence to grow the gardens and safeguard these woods in a sacred manner. Mario is among the stewards; he moved back home this year. We eagerly await the return of Jenny and her partner, Lisa, as well.

Those are my wishes after most of a lifetime on this land. If I am disabled at this point, with a bad back and other injuries from many years of physical labor; if I still do not have a washing machine, for instance, to make the workload easier; if we are still in the process of completing the structures to house the young land stewards who feel drawn here; if our dreams of establishing an eco-Indigenous community at Wild Magnolia have yet to reach full fruition; and if I have known much loss and sorrow, I hold only gratitude for a good life, a full life, a love-filled life in these sacred ancient mountains, surrounded by their beauty and riches beyond compare.

I wish to be buried on this land, a resident Ancestor in perpetuity. Until that time, I remain a Two-Spirit Rainbow Prayer Warrior, daughter of Tonantzin, and as ever, a renegade, a rebel, a survivor, a survivalist, an adventurer, a homesteader, and a matriarch. I am Águila, unapologetically, until my time in this life ends. I am already home.

Tlatzokamati.

Afterword
by Lauri Umansky

The first time I inched my Toyota Corolla up the mountain in Northwest Arkansas to visit what I thought was the lesbian land settlement Arco Iris, on a road that quickly gave way behind the Boxley Baptist Church from gravel to dirt, a road rutted at points in its three-mile incline and punctuated occasionally by colorfully woven Native American staffs and handwritten signage pointing to "La Clínica," a *man* greeted me as I entered the compound.

"I'm Arthur," he said, pulling his car alongside mine. "Welcome." A tall, shaven-headed, bearded, soft-spoken man approximately my age, he directed me to leave my overnight bag in the car and head on up into the clinic, which occupied the upper level of a refurbished barn. I took in a copious breath of winter air, clearer than anything my urban nostrils had ever encountered.

I had asked to come out to this self-described "sanctuary that empowers women and children of color" in the Ozarks to begin my research into women's land communities in Arkansas.[1] I would soon come to view Arturo (who had Anglicized his name upon our first meeting) and his cousin María Cristina Moroles, the "matriarchal steward" of Arco Iris, as close friends, even family. I had not intended for that to happen, but the story of how and why it did must be told if this book is to be understood for exactly what it is, and what it is not.

I arrived in Jonesboro, a small city in Northeast Arkansas, in May of 2012. I had been in town for just a few days when I accepted a new colleague's invitation to attend Mother's Day services at one of the larger, mainstream churches in town. Like many other people I met over my first few months as dean of the College of Humanities and Social Sciences at Arkansas State University, he had assumed that I was both Christian and churchgoing. Rather than correct him on either count, I accepted his gesture of hospitality.

Honor your mother on this day as on all days, the clean-cut, young, white male preacher told the congregation. Do, however, remember that mothers are women, and women have their place in God's design. Their place is in the home and behind the man. "The head of every man is Christ; and the head of the woman is the man." "Wives, submit yourselves unto your own husbands, as unto the Lord."

I stumbled out of church pinching myself: What century was I in? What plant was I on? In truth, the sermon should not have shocked me as much as it did. On my interview for the dean's position, another administrator had offered up a slice of advice. "Don't push," he said. "It's not feminine." I pushed hard nonetheless through my growing doubts at that point, stirred by the challenge of working in public higher education serving one of the most straitened sections of one of the most beleaguered states in the Union, the Delta region of Arkansas. Four months later, I packed my bags and left Boston, where I had lived since high school, braced to embrace the "Natural State."

What seemed to surprise many of the Arkansans I met was that I had made the move alone, leaving as one child headed off to college, the other relocated to North Carolina, and my husband prepared to retire gradually over the next two years from his work as a public defender. Imagine a fifty-two-year-old woman on her own! "When will your husband be joining you?" numerous people asked anxiously (including one, illegally, during the interview process). Whether their concern revolved around safety, or propriety, or perhaps idle curiosity, I could not tell. Breaching the borders of Arkansas as a feme sole, even in the twenty-first century, apparently caused some consternation.

This rankled. For one, it did not comport with the image of Arkansas evinced by the popular or the scholarly works I had scoured as I prepared for my big move. A late-settled southern state with swamps, wild-running rivers, and scraggly mountains, Arkansas long held a reputation befitting its early moniker, the "Bear State." Gun-toting homesteaders isolated in mountain hollows; tough-as-nails, long-bearded frontiersmen; and hillbillies marched in larger-than-life masculinist formation through my mind when I thought of early Arkansans.[2]

The little I knew about Arkansas's women's image fit this individualist model, too. Hattie Caraway rode into the US Senate in 1931 on her widow's weeds and gained reelection with more help from Huey Long than from any concerted feminist activism. A precious few other Arkansas women stood out for me, exceptional individuals who broke through the oppression of racism, sexism, poverty to share their gifts: Maya Angelou, Daisy Bates, and more dubiously, Carrie Nation, who spent her last years in Eureka Springs, of all places.[3]

Dabbling in stereotypes produces shallow understanding. Similarly, a "great man" or "great woman" approach to history yields only stories of heroic individuals who break barriers of time, place, and position. Arkansas women's history, in fact, contains its fair share of collective agitation by and for women. Indeed, Arkansas was the first US territory to pass a statute protecting married women's property rights. Arkansas women voted in party primaries as early as 1916, and the state was twelfth in the nation to ratify women's suffrage. Not too shabby, one might kvell, except that in this state's case, as in others, the rallying cry of "Votes for Women!" as often signified an attempt to thwart African Americans' progress as to promote (white) women's rights.[4]

Nor was I altogether new to the South, having spent childhood years in Charlotte, North Carolina, in the late 1960s and early '70s. And throughout my adult life, I had visited my parents as they moved around the South for work and then retirement. I therefore understood that the chivalrous door holding a "lady" received in these places, the "yes, ma'am" and "no, ma'am" conventions, did not translate generally into material advantage. On almost any measure of well-being, women in Arkansas, as in virtually all southern states, rank well below the average for the nation. Women of color fare far worse. I had not been here a day before I heard the "thank God for Mississippi" response to Arkansas's bottomed-out ranking on almost every indicator, from rates of births to teenage mothers to poverty to domestic violence to overall mortality.

All of this is complicated, or in today's parlance, comprehensible only through deep, intersectional analysis. In addition to rank sexism, consider poverty, racism, classism, ableism, ageism, political conservatism, religious fundamentalism, xenophobia, homophobia, transphobia, educational deprivation—to name a few factors—when trying to understand what it means to be a woman in this place, in these times.

By the time I had been in Arkansas for five years, I had shed the thankless role of dean to rejoin the faculty and direct an interdisciplinary doctoral program in Heritage Studies. At last, I had the relative freedom from administrative duties to pursue a new round of research. Given my longtime scholarly interest in feminism and radicalism in the US, I began to look seriously at instances of women's pushback against the oppression they so clearly faced in my adopted state. I had by then put down roots, had brought my multiracial family to the mostly red state, and wanted to focus on grassroots, collective resistance to oppression—the only kind of resistance, I had long believed, that can spark meaningful societal change or bring about social justice. I also wanted to return to a research interest I had explored in my early work: the influence of countercultural utopianism on feminist and womanist activism in the 1960s, '70s, and beyond.

Once I moved beyond my initial culture shock, I did, of course, learn that feminist and womanist activism had been a part of the Arkansas landscape for well over a century. As mothers, sisters, and daughters, as students, as workers, as lovers, as church members and clergy, as community activists, as artists and as freedom fighters—as the makers of "good trouble" in every arena—women in Arkansas had fought for their own rights and dignity as fiercely as women in any other state, at any other time. The relative paucity of scholarship in the field, and the challenges for an outsider in reading the nuances of the often rural and local activism, should in no way diminish the significance of past or present struggle toward social justice and liberation.

My ears perked up when a friend casually mentioned that the Ozarks region of Northwest Arkansas had been host to a wildflower-like uncropping of lesbian back-to-the-land ventures since the 1970s. The Arkansas these women chose to see, and some stalwarts still see, bespoke a frontier of possibility, a place of natural beauty not despoiled by "man" or men, where women of like ideals and passions could fashion a good life, a ruggedly pastoral utopia, a collective, a sisterhood. At least one of these land settlements, my friend informed me, existed explicitly as a place of refuge for women and children of color.

I began to read feverishly, refreshing my general knowledge of American utopianism, counterculturalism, communalism, the late twentieth-century back-to-the-land movement, ecofeminism, spiritual feminism, lesbian feminism in the South, and the "land-dyke" movement—as the lesbian back-to-the-land movement has been dubbed. Then I zeroed in on Arkansas, reading widely about the Ozarks region, including the vicious and intentional "racial cleansing" of the area in the late 1800s and early 1900s.[5] I read everything I could find on Arkansas women's history and activism, as on gay and lesbian history and activism in the state. Finally, I turned to sources on feminist movements in Northwest Arkansas, especially the Fayetteville area, and women's land communities in the region from the 1970s to the present.

Eventually my background research led me to focus on two intentional land settlements, both of which had sprung from the Sassafras community in Ponca, Arkansas. Sassafras began as a heterosexual commune in 1972, evolved into a lesbian separatist community, and disbanded around 1980 amidst internal strife, much of it inflected with race and class tension. The first of these spin-off communities, Arco Iris, took shape on land adjoining Sassafras, land also purchased by Sassafras founder Diana Rivers. María Cristina Moroles initiated what became known as Arco Iris in 1976. Forty years later, she remained there, in what had never been a lesbian separatist community per se, but rather a "sacred land space," principally but not exclusively for women and children of color. Closer to Fayetteville, in Madison County, Diana Rivers and nineteen other women in 1981 founded the Ozark Land Holding Association, a lesbian land community that to this day operates on what was originally one hundred forty acres of land, now doubled, near Crosses, Arkansas.[6]

Gradually, I worked my way through many of the sources available. Somewhere in the midst of all that reading and refreshing of memory, I contacted Arco Iris and OLHA for interviews. Through a series of emails and phone calls, I arranged to visit Arco Iris first, in early February of 2018.

I decided to take the more scenic northern route from Jonesboro to Ponca, skirting the Missouri border into the Ozarks, a decision that made me acutely aware of the white privilege that spirited me unnoticed through territory my Black friends and family members swore never to enter. I had been warned in particular about Harrison, a town only thirty-five miles from Arco Iris, long known as a sundown town, with a contemporary Ku Klux Klan compound nearby.[7] A smattering of Confederate flags along the route reinforced my perception of penetrating hostile territory. (On a subsequent trip a few months later, I encountered a white supremacist rally in Harrison, awash with Confederate flags, swastikas, banners quoting Bible passages, and cardboard signs denouncing LGBTQI2S people as "perverts.") The languorous beauty of the rolling hills of Boone and then Newton County could not have made the contrast more painful to behold.

On my first trip up the dirt road to Arco Iris, I took in the serenity of the winter woods, the clarity of the air, the remoteness of the settlement three miles up the mountain. This would be my first overnight stay off the grid.

An hour later, I lay mostly naked beneath a light blanket as an arrestingly tall, slim woman dressed in flowing white cotton braced by a wide, colorful woven belt, her long graying hair held back by an embroidered headband, drew her fingers lightly along my spine. I do not usually strip down to conduct interviews for my writing projects. In this case, during a phone conversation with María Cristina Moroles, we had arranged for a "treatment" during the visit, for which I would pay her regular fee. I would thus gain some insight into her work as a curandera, receive the healing she offered, and make a contribution to the community. She, in turn, could avoid being asked yet again, as she said, to tell her story for free to another white academic who would get it wrong anyway.

The treatment began with a *plática*, a talk, in which she asked me to speak about my general sense of health or well-being. Did I have concerns I wished to address? Stress and anxiety, I said. I hold it in my body; it keeps me awake at night. We talked for some time about diet, exercise, self-care. I talked about my children and grandchildren. She took notes, as any caregiver would during an intake interview.

I took mental notes myself, observing the quiet, serious-minded woman whose gaze took in, with a wry smile, my high-femme, urban appearance —blonded hair, mascara, nails, lacy dainties—but who asked neutrally about my health and worries. She spoke knowledgeably about a wide range of healing traditions and practices, expressing herself in lay terms I could understand. Though I knew a bit about her life history from the reading I had done, I got no inkling of her early streetwise Dallas days until, as I lay on the massage table, all five feet one of me, she laughed out loud at how far from the foot of the table I ended and said teasingly, "Get on down here, shorty." Polished and street; city and country; analytical and spontaneous. I knew I was going to like her.

Long into the night, María Cristina and I, at times joined by cousin Arturo, prepared and ate delicious vegetarian food and drank the Merlot I had brought, supplemented later with her homemade elderberry wine. We talked without pause. We had so much to say to each other, cover-ing bedrock areas of commonality in life experience and perspective, along with almost comical areas of difference. From a wild adolescence with little adult supervision in Dallas and Boston, respectively, and the trauma that precipitated and resulted from premature emancipation; to lifelong interest in matters feminist, countercultural, and esoteric; to familial and activist immersion in multiracial community; to amorous relationships at points in our lives with both women and men—we found much common ground.

She was an Indigenous woman with formal schooling through the seventh grade who had lived on top of a mountain for over forty years and who had spent most of her life in lesbian relationships, while I was a white woman of secular Jewish heritage with a doctorate and had lived in large northern cities and spent most of my years married to men—yet we connected in a way that happens only a few times in life. By the wee hours, when Arturo led me back to the clinic/loft where I would sleep, we had already adopted nicknames, predictable ones, for each other: Tall One and Little One.

The next morning, I asked if I could turn on the tape recorder as we continued to talk. At first, I directed questions toward the period of time when Arco Iris emerged from Sassafras, trying to get my grounding in what was then taking shape in my mind—based on my recent reading, previous research, and personal experience in feminist movements over several decades—to be a rural, southern example of the ruptures within US women's movements of the 1970s over matters of racism and classism, not to mention lesbian separatism.[8]

"That all happened after I died," María Cristina explained. "When I came back as SunHawk."

As I listened for several hours, she spoke of the spiritual journey that brought her to the land, through dreams, visions, and guidance from wise elders. She spoke of her "sacred responsibility" to protect the land and all of its inhabitants—plant, animal, and human. She spoke of her own trauma and healing, over decades and through multiple modalities. She spoke with urgency and fluidity, straying far from what I had thought to be the topic at hand. Somehow, I knew not to stop her. Several times, each of us, for our own reasons, said, "This story needs to be told."

By the time I left Arco Iris the next morning, we had resolved that our work together would transcend María Cristina's contribution to my wider study of women's land settlements in Northwest Arkansas. I pledged to work with her to write and publish her story, her memoir.

"First I'll complete the other project, where your story is only one piece of the whole and the whole is only one piece of your story," I said.

Over the next couple of months, I returned to Northwest Arkansas several times to interview Nancy Vaughn and Diana Rivers about OLHA, with the original project still in mind. I disclosed to Vaughn and Rivers that I had interviewed and befriended María Cristina. They spoke generously and frankly on tape, and for the record. At several points, I interviewed

Isis (Sheila Brown) at Arco Iris. Meanwhile, I continued to interview María Cristina in an open-ended way, ultimately recording about fifty hours of interviews. As that corpus of material grew, my objectivity waned beyond any point of recovery. I finally conceded to myself that a scholarly treatment of the complex, and at times acrimonious, history of Sassafras, Arco Iris, and OLHA would need to be researched and written by someone else.

Toward that end, we offer this volume as a primary source. We also include here a bibliography of the background sources I scoured as I delved into the project as originally conceived. These works eventually came to include readings in recent Native American and Latinx history, along with books on shamanism and *curanderismo*, as I sharpened my focus on María Cristina's life story.

What nature of beast, then, is this book? It cannot be called a work of conventional scholarship; it does not pretend to be that. Nor does it quite fit the mold of "testimonial" literature, wherein a person who is structurally cut off from channels of communication and influence tells her story through someone who does have access to those resources. María Cristina Moroles, should she have chosen to do so, could have written and published a memoir without my involvement. It would have been a different book, to be sure.

This book reflects a collaborative process. The process involved a deep dive into memory for María Cristina. She revisited, and spoke of, the experiences of a lifetime. Some she recalled for the first time in many years. Some she spoke out loud for the first time ever. Some she had told over and over, and not always in the same way, depending on audience and circumstances. These pages reflect the memories she wants to tell at this moment in her life, in as full or as truncated a form as she believes will preserve her story for posterity. I believe that she has told her truth as she understands it now, from the vantage point of seven decades of living.

This is always true of memoir, as of memory. We bring to it experiences we have encountered, reshaping our understanding of those experiences all the while. There is no static moment of original truth in memory, or in memoir. Beyond a few historical signposts, it cannot be "fact-checked." Nor should it be. It is an exercise in creative nonfiction, truthful but also molded into a narrative.

Our practical process in writing the book went something like this: First I transcribed all of the tapes. This took many months of close work, much of it coinciding with my quarantining at home during the COVID-19 pandemic. Then, working with the transcribed material, I drafted sections of the narrative, using as much of María Cristina's actual wording as possible. Spoken word differs from written word at every level of structure, however, complicating the matter of "authorship" from the start. As I completed sections, I sent them to María Cristina. Did this section say what she wanted it to say? Did the words feel right to her? She made many corrections, some of fact and some of sequence or tone or nuance. Each segment passed back and forth between us several times until it felt just right to her.

Occasionally we recorded a new session to fill in detail that our initial round of interviews somehow missed. María Cristina also sent writings she had done over the years: poems, prayers, blessings, ceremonies, recipes, eulogies. We worked some of these into the manuscript where we felt they belonged.

We included as many photographs as our publisher allowed, trying to give readers a fuller sense of the people, places, animals, and plants that populate the narrative. The photo essay about Sheila "Isis" Brown in her final days, through death and burial, we included at the explicit request of Isis upon diagnosis of her terminal illness.

I tried to stay out of the way in the telling of María Cristina's story. Recognizing the fallacy of that invisibility, however, I have shared in this postscript some of the experiences and perspectives that brought me to our collaborative work. We will leave it for readers, scholars, critics, and the future to name the genre, if they must. Is it an as-told-to memoir? Is it a coauthored work of creative nonfiction? Yes and yes, I would say. For me, the book is a gift to a treasured friend as she works through the meaning of her time in this life. I believe that she has told her story with integrity and valor. It is a unique story of profound depth, written in the Book of Life for the ages, and preserved here in these pages.

In María Cristina's words:

I share here my story of waking up to remember our sacredness and the universal laws given to us, the original Indigenous people, by the Creator, telling us to protect our Mother Earth, protect the old, young, poor, and vulnerable. I pray that my story gives others courage to face the challenges of these crucial, changing times. I share my story to demonstrate that we can rise above our oppressors' theft of positions of power and leadership, of resources, of the very land, our Mother Earth, and all Her bounty. It is our time as Indigenous women to speak out. We must act NOW for the survival of our Indigenous peoples, our sisters, our children, and our planet, Mother Earth.

Notes

1. "Arco Iris Earth Care Project," https://www.arcoirisearthcareproject.com, accessed January 24, 2021.

2. Brooks Blevins, *Arkansaw/Arkansas: How Bear Hunters, Hillbillies, and Good Ol' Boys Defined a State* (Fayetteville: University of Arkansas Press, 2009); and Blevins, *Hill Folks: A History of Arkansas Ozarkers and Their Image* (Chapel Hill: University of North Carolina Press, 2002).

3. Cherisse Jones-Branch and Gary T. Edwards, eds., *Arkansas Women: Their Lives and Times* (Athens: University of Georgia Press, 2018); Fran Grace, *Carry A. Nation: Retelling the Life* (Bloomington: Indiana University Press, 2001); and Nancy Hendricks, *Notable Women of Arkansas: From Hattie to Hillary, 100 Names to Know* (Little Rock: Butler Center Books, 2016).

4. *Arkansas Women's Suffrage Centennial* virtual exhibit, University of Arkansas at Little Rock Center for Arkansas History and Culture, http://ualrexhibits.org/suffrage/ (accessed January 20, 2021); Bernadette Cahill, *Arkansas Women and the Right to Vote: The Little Rock Campaigns, 1868–1920* (Little Rock: Butler Center Books, 2015); Michael B. Dougan, "The Arkansas Married Woman's Property Law," *Arkansas Historical Quarterly* 46 (Spring 1987): 3–26; and Louise M. Newman, *White Women's Rights: The Racial Origins of Feminism in the United States* (New York: Oxford University Press, 1999).

5. Kimberly Harper, *White Man's Heaven: The Lynching and Expulsion of Blacks in the Southern Ozarks, 1894–1909* (Fayetteville: University of Arkansas Press, 2010); and Guy Lancaster, *Racial Cleansing in Arkansas, 1883–1924: Politics, Land, Labor, and Criminality* (Lanham, MD: Lexington Books, 2014).

6. Joyce Cheney, ed., *Lesbian Land* (Minneapolis: Word Weavers, 1985); Jordan Gass-Poore, "Lesbian-Only 'Intentional Community' Outlasts Others," *Arkansas Democrat-Gazette*, August 31, 2015, pp. 1A and 6A; Rose Norman, Merril Mushroom, and Kate Ellison, eds., *Landykes of the South: Women's Land Groups and Lesbian Communities in the South*, in *Sinister Wisdom* 98 (New York: A Midsummer Night's Press, 2015); and Anna M. Zajicek, Allyn Lord, and Lori Holyfield, "The Emergence and First Years of a Grassroots Women's Movement in Northwest Arkansas, 1970–1980," *Arkansas Historical Quarterly* 62 (Summer 2003): 153–81.

7. Jacqueline Froelich, "Race, History, and Memory in Harrison, Arkansas: An Ozarks Town Reckons with Its Past," in *Race and Ethnicity in Arkansas: New Perspectives*, ed. John A. Kirk (Fayetteville: University of Arkansas Press, 2014); Jacqueline Froelich and David Zimmerman, "Total Eclipse: The Destruction of the African American Community of Harrison, Arkansas, in 1905 and 1909," *Arkansas Historical Quarterly* 58 (Summer 1999): 131–59; and Harper, *White Man's Heaven*.

8. See, for example, Alice Echols, *Daring to Be Bad: Radical Feminism in America, 1967–1975* (Minneapolis: University of Minnesota Press, 1989); also, Lauri Umansky, *Motherhood Reconceived: Feminism and the Legacies of the Sixties* (New York: New York University Press, 1996).

Selected Bibliography

Agigian, Amy. *Baby Steps: How Lesbian Alternative Insemination Is Changing the World.* Middletown, CT: Wesleyan University Press, 2006.

Agnew, Eleanor. *Back from the Land: How Young Americans Went to Nature in the 1970s, and Why They Came Back.* Chicago: Ivan R. Dee, 2004.

Anzaldúa, Gloria. *Borderlands / La Frontera: The New Mestiza.* San Francisco: Aunt Lute Books, 2012.

Arms, Suzanne. *Immaculate Deception: A New Look at Women and Childbirth.* New York: Bantam, 1981.

Avila, Elena, and Joy Parker. *Woman Who Glows in the Dark: A Curandera Reveals Traditional Aztec Secrets of Physical and Spiritual Health.* New York: Tarcher/Putnam, 2000.

Bammer, Angelika. *Partial Visions: Feminism and Utopianism in the 1970s.* New York: Routledge, 1991.

Blevins, Brooks. *Arkansas/Arkansaw: How Bear Hunters, Hillbillies, and Good Ol' Boys Defined a State.* Fayetteville: University of Arkansas Press, 2009.

———. *Hill Folks: A History of Arkansas Ozarkers and Their Image.* Chapel Hill: University of North Carolina Press, 2002.

Brown, Dona. *Back to the Land: The Enduring Dream of Self-Sufficiency in Modern America.* Madison: University of Wisconsin Press, 2011.

Buenaflor, Erika. *Cleansing Rites of Curanderismo: Limpias Espirituales of Ancient Mesoamerican Shamans.* Rochester, VT: Bear and Co., 2018.

Cahill, Bernadette. *Arkansas Women and the Right to Vote: The Little Rock Campaigns, 1868–1920.* Little Rock: Butler Center Books, 2015.

Caldecott, Leone, and Stephanie LeLand. *Reclaim the Earth: Women Speak Out for Life on Earth.* London: Women's Press, 1983.

Calderón, Eduardo, Richard Cowan, Douglas Sharon, and F. Kaye Sharon. *Eduardo el Curandero: The Words of a Peruvian Healer.* Berkeley, CA: North Atlantic Books, 1982.

Cantú, Norma Elia. *Canícula: Snapshots of a Girlhood en La Frontera.* Albuquerque: University of New Mexico Press, 1995.

Carson, Rachel. *Silent Spring.* New York: Fawcett, 1962.

Chacaby, Ma-Nee, with Mary Luisa Plummer. *A Two-Spirit Journey: The Autobiography of a Lesbian Ojibwa-Cree Elder.* Winnipeg: University of Manitoba Press, 2016.

Cheney, Joyce. *Lesbian Land.* Minneapolis: Word Weavers, 1985.

Cox, Craig. *Storefront Revolution: Food Co-ops and the Counterculture.* New Brunswick, NJ: Rutgers University Press, 1996.

Dews, Carlos L., and Carolyn Leste Law. *Out in the South.* Philadelphia: Temple University Press, 2001.

Diamond, Irene, and Gloria Feman Orenstein, eds. *Reweaving the World: The Emergence of Ecofeminism*. San Francisco: Sierra Club Books, 1990.

Diamond, Stephen. *What the Trees Said: Life on a New Age Farm*. New York: Dell, 1971.

Dobbyn, Dorothy. "A Feminist's Case for Homebirth." *Women: A Journal of Liberation* 4, no. 3 (1976): 20–23.

Dougan, Michael B. "The Arkansas Married Woman's Property Law." *Arkansas Historical Quarterly* 46 (Spring 1987): 3–26.

Dunbar-Ortiz, Roxanne. *An Indigenous Peoples' History of the United States*. Boston: Beacon, 2014.

Echols, Alice. *Daring to Be Bad: Radical Feminism in America, 1967–1975*. Minneapolis: University of Minnesota Press, 1989.

Ehrenreich, Barbara, and Deirdre English. *Witches, Midwives, and Nurses: A History of Women Healers*. Old Westbury, NY: Feminist Press, 1973.

Ellison, Kate. "Lesbian Land: An Overview." *Alternatives* (May–June 2003): 39–41.

Enzer, Julie. "Night Heron Press and Lesbian Print Culture in North Carolina, 1976–1983." *Southern Cultures* 21, no. 2 (Summer 2015): 43–56.

Evins, Janie S. "Arkansas Women: Their Contributions to Society, Politics, and Business." *Arkansas Historical Quarterly* 44 (Summer 1985): 118–33.

Froelich, Jacqueline, and David Zimmerman. "Total Eclipse: The Destruction of the African American Community of Harrison, Arkansas, in 1905 and 1909." *Arkansas Historical Quarterly* 58 (Summer 1999): 131–59.

Gaskin, Ina May. *Spiritual Midwifery*. Summertown, TN: The Book Publishing Company, 1977.

Giddings, Paula. *When and Where I Enter: The Impact of Black Women on Race and Sex in America*. New York: Bantam Books, 1985.

Gould, Rebecca Kneale. *At Home in Nature: Modern Homesteading and Spiritual Practice in America*. Berkeley: University of California Press, 2005.

Hanscombe, Gillian E., and Jackie Forster. *Rocking the Cradle: Lesbian Mothers; A Challenge in Family Living*. Boston: Alyson Publications, 1982.

Harker, Jaime. *The Lesbian South: Southern Feminists, the Women in Print Movement, and the Queer Literary Canon*. Chapel Hill: University of North Carolina Press, 2018.

Harper, Kimberly. *White Man's Heaven: The Lynching and Expulsion of Blacks in the Southern Ozarks, 1894–1909*. Fayetteville: University of Arkansas Press, 2010.

Harris, Adrienne, and Ynestra King, eds. *Rocking the Ship of State: Toward a Feminist Peace Politics*. Boulder, CO: Westview, 1989.

Heart, Bear, and Molly Larkin. *The Wind Is My Mother: The Life and Teachings of a Native American Shaman*. New York: Penguin, 1996.

Hedgepeth, William, and Dennis Stock. *The Alternative: Communal Life in New America*. London: Macmillan, 1970.

Hendricks, Nancy. *Notable Arkansas Women: From Hattie to Hillary, 100 Names to Know*. Little Rock: Butler Center Books, 2016.

Hitchens, Donna, and Ann Thomas, eds. *Lesbian Mothers and Their Children: An Annotated Bibliography of Legal and Psychological Materials*. San Francisco: Lesbian Rights Project, 1980.

Holloway, Pippa. "Manifesto for a Queer South Politics." *Publications of the Modern Language Association of America* 131, no. 1 (2016): 182–86.

hooks, bell. *Ain't I a Woman? Black Women and Feminism*. Boston: South End Press, 1981.

———. *Feminist Theory: From Margin to Center*. Boston: South End Press, 1984.

———. *Talking Back: Thinking Feminist, Thinking Black*. Boston: South End Press, 1989.

Howard, John, ed. *Carryin' On in the Lesbian South*. New York: New York University Press, 1997.

Hutchens, Alma R. *Indian Herbalogy of North America*. Boston: Shambhala Publications, 1991.

Jacobs, Jeffrey. *New Pioneers: The Back-to-the-Land Movement and the Search for a Sustainable Future*. University Park: Pennsylvania State University Press, 1997.

Jacobs, Sue-Ellen, Wesley Thomas, and Sabine Lang, eds. *Two-Spirit People: Native American Gender Identity, Sexuality, and Spirituality*. Champaign: University of Illinois Press, 1997.

Jacoway, Elizabeth, ed. *Behold, Our Works Were Good: A Handbook of Arkansas Women's History*. Little Rock: August House, 1988.

Jaspin, Elliot. *Buried in the Bitter Waters: The Hidden History of Racial Cleansing in America*. New York: Basic Books, 2007.

Jobes, Patrick C. *Moving Nearer to Heaven: The Illusions and Disillusions of Migrants to Scenic Rural Places*. Westport, CT: Praeger, 2000.

Johnson, Ben F. *Arkansas in Modern America, 1930–1999*. Fayetteville: University of Arkansas Press, 2000.

Jones-Branch, Cherisse, and Gary T. Edwards, eds. *Arkansas Women: Their Lives and Times*. Athens: University of Georgia Press, 2018.

Kalweit, Holger. *Shamans, Healers, and Medicine Men*. Boston: Shambhala, 2000.

Kendall, Laurie J. *The Michigan Womyn's Music Festival: An Amazon Matrix of Meaning*. Baltimore: The Spiral Womyn's Press, 2013.

Kersen, Thomas Michael. *Where Misfits Fit: Counterculture and Influence in the Ozarks*. Jackson: University Press of Mississippi, 2021.

Kloss, Jethro. *Back To Eden*. 5th ed. Santa Barbara, CA: Woodbridge Press Publishing Company, 1975.

Lancaster, Guy. *Racial Cleansing in Arkansas, 1883–1924: Politics, Land, Labor, and Criminality*. Lanham, MD: Lexington Books, 2014.

Lavelle, Janelle. "Lesbian Land." *Southern Exposure* 16, no. 3 (1988): 36–38.

Loewen, James W. *Sundown Towns: A Hidden Dimension of American Racism.* New York: The New Press, 2005.

Lord, Allyn, and Anna M. Zajicek. *The History of the Contemporary Grassroots Women's Movement in Northwest Arkansas, 1970–2000.* Fayetteville, AR: University of Arkansas, 2000.

Lorde, Audre. *Sister, Outsider: Essays and Speeches.* Trumansberg, NY: Crossing Press, 1984.

Luis, Kerdwen N. "Ourlands: Culture, Gender, and Intention in Women's Land Communities in the United States." PhD diss., Brandeis University, 2009.

Lynn, Jessica Louise. "Country Women: Back-to-the-Land Feminism and Radical Feminist Praxis in the Women's Liberation Movement." Master's thesis, Southern Illinois University, 2013.

Matsuda, Mari J. "The West and the Legal Status of Women: Expectations of Frontier Feminism." *Journal of the West* 24 (January 1985): 47–52.

McAllister, Pam, ed. *Reweaving the Web of Life: Feminism and Nonviolence.* Philadelphia: New Society, 1982.

McGowan, Morgan Gray. "This Is Lesbian Land: What Family Means for a Lesbian Intentional Community." PhD diss., University of Louisiana at Monroe, 2020.

McNeil, W. K. *Ozark Country.* Jackson: University Press of Mississippi, 1995.

Melville, Keith. *Communes in the Counterculture: Origins, Theories, Styles of Life.* New York: Morrow, 1972.

Miller, Timothy. *The 60s Communes: Hippies and Beyond.* Syracuse, NY: Syracuse University Press, 1999.

Mims, La Shonda. *Drastic Dykes and Accidental Activists: Queer Women in the Urban South.* Chapel Hill: University of North Carolina Press, 2022.

Montrie, Chad. *The Myth of Silent Spring: Rethinking the Origins of American Environmentalism.* Berkeley: University of California Press, 2018.

Moraga, Cherríe L. *Loving in the War Years: Lo Que Nunca Pasó Por Sus Labios.* Boston: South End Press, 1983.

———— and Gloria Anzaldúa, eds. *This Bridge Called My Back: Writings by Radical Women of Color.* New York: Kitchen Table / Women of Color Press, 1981.

Nearing, Helen, and Scott Nearing. *Living the Good Life: How to Live Sanely and Simply in a Troubled World.* New York: Schocken Books, 1970.

Newell, Leslie, and Frank Schambach. *Crossroads of the Past: 12,000 Years of Indian Life in Arkansas.* Little Rock: Arkansas Humanities Council, 1990.

Norman, Rose, Merril Mushroom, and Kate Ellison, eds. *Landykes of the South: Women's Land Groups and Lesbian Communities in the South. Sinister Wisdom* 98. New York: A Midsummer Night's Press, 2015.

Parker, Suzi. *Sex in the South: Unbuckling the Bible Belt*. New York: Justin, Charles, and Co., 2003.

Perrone, Bobette, H. Henrietta Stockel, and Victoria Krueger. *Medicine Women, Curanderas, and Women Doctors*. Norman: University of Oklahoma Press, 1989.

Phillips, Jared M. "Hipbillies and Hillbillies: Back-to-the-Landers in the Arkansas Ozarks during the 1970s." *Arkansas Historical Quarterly* 75 (Summer 2016): 89–110.

———. *Hipbillies: Deep Revolution in the Arkansas Ozarks*. Fayetteville: University of Arkansas Press, 2019.

Plant, Judith. *Healing the Wounds: The Promise of Ecofeminism*. Philadelphia: New Society, 1989.

Plaskow, Judith, and Carol P. Christ, eds. *Weaving the Visions: New Patterns in Feminist Spirituality*. San Francisco: Harper and Row, 1989.

Quesada, Uriel, Letitia Gómez, and Salvador Vidal-Ortiz, eds. *Queer Brown Voices: Personal Narratives of Latina/o LGBT Activism*. Austin: University of Texas Press, 2015.

Rafferty, Milton D. *The Ozarks: Land and Life*. 2nd ed. Fayetteville: University of Arkansas Press, 2001.

Rivers, Diana. *Clouds of War*. Ferndale, MI: Bella Books, 2002.

———. *Daughters of the Great Star*. West Plains, MO: HandMaid Books, 1992.

———. *The Hadra*. Boston: Lace Publications, 1995.

———. *Her Sister's Keeper*. Tallahassee, FL: Bella Books, 2008.

———. *Journey to Zelindar*. Boston: Lace Publications, 1987.

———. *The Red Line of Yarmald*. Ferndale, MI: Bella Books, 2003.

———. *The Smuggler, The Spy, and The Spider*. Tallahassee, FL: Bella Books, 2012.

Roberts, Ron E. *The New Communes: Coming Together in America*. Englewood Cliffs, NJ: Prentice Hall, 1971.

Rothman, Barbara. *Recreating Motherhood: Ideology and Technology in a Patriarchal Society*. New York: Norton, 1989.

Schumacher, E. F. *Small Is Beautiful: Economics As If People Mattered*. New York: Schocken Books, 1975.

Segrest, Mab. *My Mama's Dead Squirrel: Lesbian Essays on Southern Culture*. Ithaca, NY: Firebrand, 1985.

Sherman, Jory. *My Heart Is in the Ozarks*. Harrison, AR: First Ozark Press, 1982.

Shi, David. *The Simple Life: Plain Living and High Thinking in American Culture*. Athens: University of Georgia Press, 2007.

Smith, Barbara, ed. *Home Girls: A Black Feminist Anthology*. New York: Kitchen Table Press, 1983.

Smith, Sherry L. *Hippies, Indians, and the Fight for Red Power*. Oxford: Oxford University Press, 2012.

Stockley, Grif. *Daisy Bates: Civil Rights Crusader from Arkansas*. Jackson: University Press of Mississippi, 2005.

Starhawk. *The Spiral Dance: A Rebirth of the Ancient Religion of the Great Goddess.* San Francisco: Harper, 1999.

Stone, Jayme Millsap. " 'They Were Her Daughters': Women and Grassroots Organizing for Social Justice in the Arkansas Delta, 1870–1970." PhD diss., University of Memphis, 2010.

Sutton, Leslie, Parr Sutton, and Maribeth Lynes. *Visits with Ozark Country Women.* Little Rock, AR: August House, 1979.

Taylor, Elizabeth A. "The Woman Suffrage Movement in Arkansas." *Arkansas Historical Quarterly* 15 (Spring 1956): 17–52.

Tedlock, Barbara. *The Woman in the Shaman's Body: Reclaiming the Feminine in Religion and Medicine.* New York: Bantam, 2005.

Tettrault, Jeanne, and Sherry Thomas. *Country Women: A Handbook for the New Farmer.* New York: Anchor Press, 1976.

Thompson, Brock. *The Un-Natural State: Arkansas and the Queer South.* Fayetteville: University of Arkansas Press, 2010.

Torres, Eliseo, and Timothy L. Sawyer. *Curandero: A Life in Mexican Folk Healing.* Albuquerque: University of New Mexico Press, 2005.

Trujillo, Carla. *Chicana Lesbians: The Girls Our Mothers Warned Us About.* San Antonio, TX: Third Woman Press, 1991.

Umansky, Lauri. *Motherhood Reconceived: Feminism and the Legacies of the Sixties.* New York: New York University Press, 1996.

Vida, Virginia, ed. *Our Right to Love: A Lesbian Resource Book.* Englewood Cliffs, NJ: Prentice Hall, 1978.

Warren, Patricia Nell. *One Is the Sun.* Glendale, CA: Wildcat Press, 1991.

Weinstein, Ruth. *A Force for Social Change: Ozark Back-to-the-Land Settlements, 1970–1975.* Little Rock: Arkansas Humanities Council, 1996.

Whayne, Jeannie M., et al. *Arkansas: A Narrative History.* Fayetteville: University of Arkansas Press, 2002.

Zajicek, Anna M., Allyn Lord, and Lori Holyfield. "The Emergence and First Years of a Grassroots Women's Movement in Northwest Arkansas, 1970–1980." *Arkansas Historical Quarterly* 62 (Summer 2003): 153–81.

About the Authors

María Cristina Moroles is matriarch of Arco Iris, a healing sanctuary in the Ozark Mountains originally established for women and children of color and the queer community and now open to all people seeking healing. Moroles lives on the five-hundred-acre wilderness preserve in community with her children, Jennifer and Mario; visiting students; and other resident stewards. Also known by the ceremonial name Águila, she incorporates her Indigenous and Mexican American heritage in her work as a curandera, master massage therapist, and shaman. She is co-founder of the Arco Iris Earth Care Project.

Lauri Umansky teaches history and directs the Heritage Studies PhD Program at Arkansas State University. Her books include *Motherhood Reconceived: Feminism and the Legacies of the Sixties*, *Naked Is the Best Disguise* (pseud. Lauri Lewin), *"Bad" Mothers: The Politics of Blame in Twentieth-Century America*, *Impossible to Hold: Women and Culture in the 1960s*, and *The New Disability History: American Perspectives*.